"Steve Pardue brings years of meditation and research on humility to bear in this incredibly clear, rich, accessible, and practical guide. He not only clarifies what humility is through thoughtful engagement with Scripture and the Christian tradition but also shows in a compelling way how cultivating humility helps us navigate modern issues like interreligious dialogue and information overload. Pardue is a very wise guide, and I highly recommend his brief but deep book."

—UCHE ANIZOR, Professor of Theology, Talbot School of Theology, Biola University

"In *Retrieving Humility*, Dr. Pardue skillfully weaves together voices from church history, philosophy, and Scripture as he explores the inward and outward tensions that arise in our understanding and pursuit of humility. With both scholarly depth and pastoral warmth, he offers insights that challenge the mind and nourish the soul. This book will be a delight to both the thoughtful scholar and the casual reader alike."

—CHAD WILLIAMS, Senior Pastor, Union Church of Manila

"Once there was no humility. Then Jesus and the Christian movement instilled humility at the center of public virtue. More recently, discontents have raised a number of serious charges against humility even as wider culture devalues it. Steve Pardue helps all of us retrieve the true nature of humility modelled on Christ's own and to learn from responding to its varied critics."

—MICHAEL ALLEN, John Dyer Trimble Professor of Systematic Theology, Reformed Theological Seminary, Orlando

"*Retrieving Humility* is a timely and thoughtful work that brings together theological depth and pastoral insight with remarkable balance. Grounded in Scripture and enriched by the wisdom of the early church, Stephen T. Pardue calls the global church to rediscover humility as a Christ-shaped way of life. This is not an appeal to passivity, but an invitation to a posture formed by Jesus that nurtures faithful discipleship, sustains courageous witness, and restores communities fractured by pride and fear. Written with care and precision, the book speaks across cultures and ministry contexts. It will serve pastors, leaders, students, and believers who seek to follow Christ with conviction, gentleness, and integrity, offering a vision of faith that is both truthful and transformative."

—Finny Philip, Vice President, Filadelfia Bible College, Udaipur, India

"Over the years, many people have asked me to recommend a book that could serve as an 'antidote' to pride. While we have access to profound wisdom from both Scripture and church history, these insights often require a bridge to help them speak clearly to the challenges of our times. I have finally found a book that does exactly that. It draws from some of the best biblical and historical sources while grappling with the real-world complexities of humility and pride—particularly within the Christian experience. Whether you tend to take humility for granted or view it with suspicion, this book will reawaken your interest in the virtue and highlight its essential role in both faithful discipleship and bearing joyful witness to the gospel."

—Beatrice Victoria Ang, Director, Center for Theological Inquiry in Asia

Retrieving Humility

Retrieving Humility

Ancient Christian Wisdom for Modern Discipleship

STEPHEN T. PARDUE

CASCADE *Books* • Eugene, Oregon

RETRIEVING HUMILITY
Ancient Christian Wisdom for Modern Discipleship

Cascade Books
An Imprint of Wipf and Stock Publishers
199 W. 8th Ave., Suite 3
Eugene, OR 97401

www.wipfandstock.com

PAPERBACK ISBN: 978-1-7252-5463-3
HARDCOVER ISBN: 978-1-7252-5464-0
EBOOK ISBN: 978-1-7252-5465-7

Cataloguing-in-Publication data:

Names: Pardue, Stephen T., author.

Title: Retrieving humility : ancient Christian wisdom for modern discipleship / Stephen T. Pardue.

Description: Eugene, OR: Cascade Books, 2026 | Includes bibliographical references and index.

Identifiers: ISBN 978-1-7252-5463-3 (paperback) | ISBN 978-1-7252-5464-0 (hardcover) | ISBN 978-1-7252-5465-7 (ebook)

Subjects: LCSH: Humilty. | Humility—Religious aspects—Christianity.

Classification: BV4647.H8 P45 2026 (paperback) | BV4647.H8 (ebook)

03/04/26

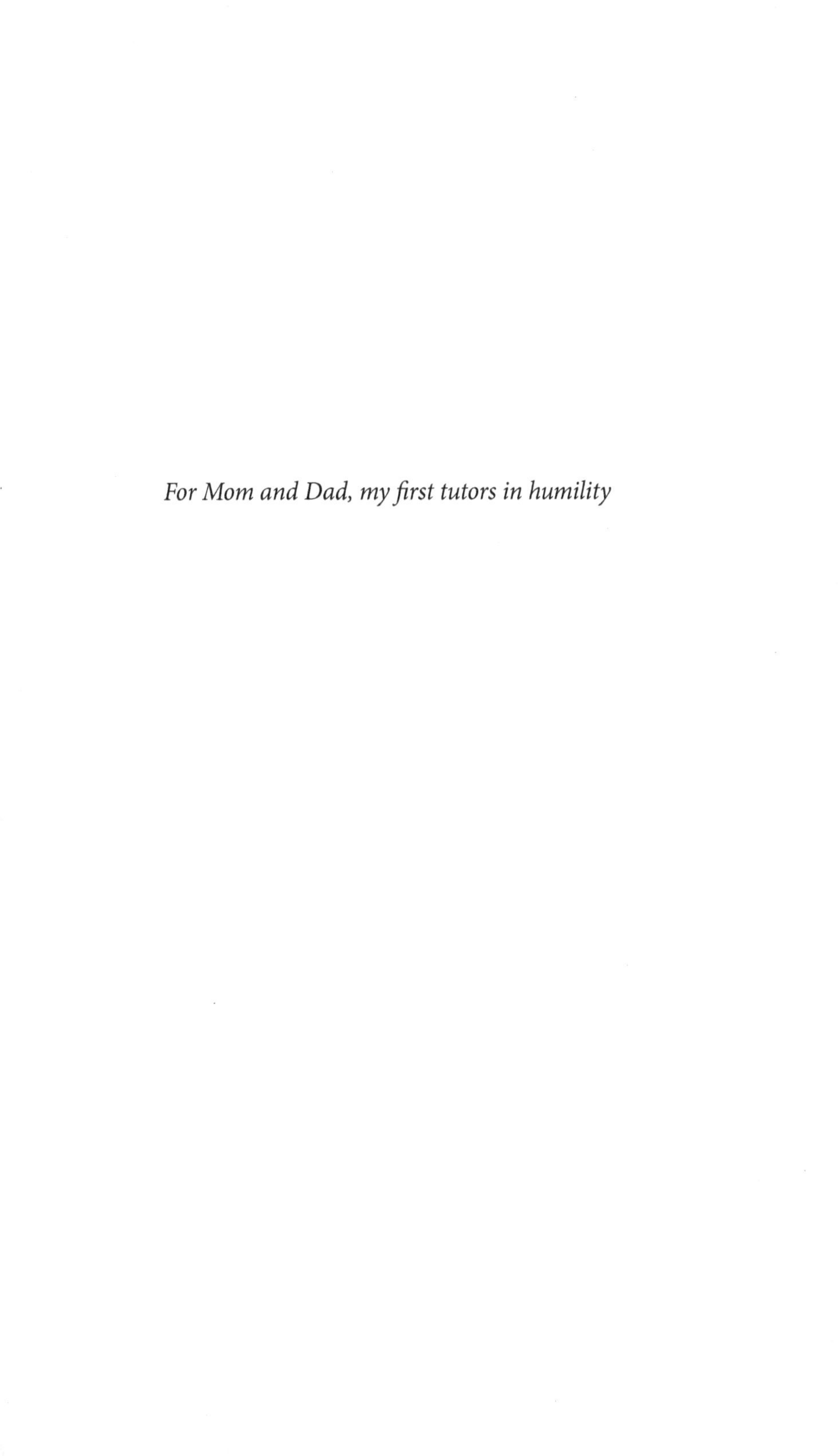

For Mom and Dad, my first tutors in humility

Contents

Acknowledgments ix

Abbreviations xi

Introduction xiii

Chapter 1 Against Humility 1
Understanding the Virtue's Critics

Chapter 2 The God Who Swings Low 16
How Christ-Shaped Humility Changes Everything

Chapter 3 Weighing Our Worth 33
Humility, Self-Esteem, and Following Jesus

Chapter 4 Humble Confidence 50
Understanding Humility and Religious Conviction

Chapter 5 Constraining Curiosity 66
How Humility Can Help Us Survive the New Information Age

Conclusion: Learning to Bake Humble Pie 83

Bibliography 101

Acknowledgments

THIS BOOK HAS BEEN long in the making, and perhaps this is fitting given that it focuses on a virtue whose development is characteristically unhurried. Along the way, I fear I have accumulated far too many debts to recall and name here, but I shall try nevertheless. The book had its initial stage of development during a research fellowship at Biola University's Center for Christian Thought, which was made possible through the support of a grant from the John Templeton Foundation. I am grateful for the support and sharpening I received during that initial season, especially from Thomas Crisp, Gregg Ten Elshof, Steve Porter, Evan Rosa, Kent Dunnington, Laura Smit, Adam Johnson, Peter Meilander, Darian Lockett, Michelle Barnewall, Doug Geivett, and Mike Erre.

As the project continued to emerge after my return to Manila, the faculty of the International Graduate School of Leadership were crucial dialogue partners. Thanks especially to President Emeritus Tom Roxas, Adam Day, Ron Barber, Andrew Heyd, Suzanne Heyd, and Mona Bias for their help refining the ideas in the book. Craig Thompson was a crucial partner keeping me going as we weathered the ups and downs of life during the chaotic pandemic lockdown years. Abraham Joseph, Theresa Lua, and Andrew Spurgeon were not only supportive bosses but also important dialogue partners and examples to learn from. Chad Williams and the saints at Union Church of Manila, including our small group, have nourished and sustained this project through their faithfulness to the humble Christ. Dan Treier, Uche Anizor, James Harnett, and Phil Smith read portions of the manuscript at various points and provided feedback that improved it substantially. Euntaek David Shin and Esther Waldrop read the final manuscript and refined it at many key points, leaving me in their debt. My thanks to Michael Thomson for believing in this project and the team at Cascade for shepherding it along. Of course, errors in the book are my own and should not reflect on any of these good people.

More than anyone else, Teri kept me chipping away at this book when I was discouraged, and I'm grateful for her feedback on early chapters, which helped shape the project. Along with our four kids, she knows more than anyone on this planet how much I need to grow in the things that I write about here. Thanks to Ava, Lucy, Simon, and Ivy, I never lacked for levity even on the most challenging writing days.

I dedicate this book to Mom and Dad, who introduced me to the humble Savior not only in what they taught but in how they lived. For as long as I've been alive, I've been drawn to the humility of Christ by their example of faithful service to God and others. They have shown me and others in real life what it means to have "the mind of Christ" (1 Cor 2:16; Phil 2:5).

Easter 2025

Abbreviations

1 Clem.	1 Clement
2 Apol.	*Second Apology*
BECNT	Baker Exegetical Commentary on the New Testament
NICOT	New International Commentary on the Old Testament
NPNF[1]	*A Select Library of Nicene and Post-Nicene Fathers of the Christian Church.* Edited by Philip Schaff. 1st ser. 14 vols. Repr., Peabody, MA: Hendrickson, 1994
SJT	*Scottish Journal of Theology*

Introduction

I DON'T REMEMBER A time before I had an interest in humility. In Sunday school lessons and sermons, I learned as a child that "God opposes the proud but gives grace to the humble" (Jas 4:6). I noticed in the Bible that God's interactions with his people often followed a pattern of exalting the overlooked and marginalized. The young and disregarded David is plucked from obscurity to become the greatest king of Israel. Mary is trusted to bear the Son of God despite her low social status and tender age. And then there is the most stunning act of humility ever known to the created order: the Son of God abandoning his status in glory to become servant and Savior.

These stories resonated with me. Maybe I identified with the underdogs, being the youngest in my family and the slowest one on the playground, and often experiencing the perpetual sense of not belonging that is common to immigrants and expatriates. Probably more importantly, I saw humility at work in my parents and the other adults in our growing evangelical Filipino Christian community. There, I caught a clear vision for how humility could solve otherwise intractable conflicts, demolishing injured pride and healing layers of shame. I saw people abandon addiction and heal deep wounds as they stopped fighting and instead embraced humble submission to Jesus. I saw in my parents a strikingly consistent posture of service to others that permeated their every waking moment, and I knew instinctively that humility was a trait worth pursuing.

These experiences were by no means unique to me. Despite rumors of humility's demise, most modern people admire humility in others and seek to cultivate it in themselves.[1] Still, I count myself lucky to have had such a personal taste from my earliest days of the centrality of humility in God's design for his people and the remarkable power it had for transforming lives.

But I also ran into some real puzzles. For example: I learned in Scripture that Jesus was a paragon of humility, demoting himself from glory in the incarnation and embracing a life of service and even humiliation on behalf of others. But I also noticed the constant refrains in the Gospels that Jesus stood out for teaching "with authority," and read the stories of him issuing extremely strong condemnations against the Pharisees and others. These actions, at least on the surface, did not seem particularly humble.

I also wondered about Jesus's state of mind. We normally think of humility as involving some kind of caution about our confidence level—a kind of modest self-evaluation that makes us ready to accept the possibility that we might be wrong. But it didn't make sense to me that Jesus might ever experience this, given his divine perfection and knowing all things. And so I wondered: How could he embody humility at all, let alone perfectly?

These puzzles kept coming. As I grew older and learned about the concept of self-esteem, I came to recognize a tension between this apparently key marker of mental health and the virtue that I had learned to admire. Later, when I became a parent, I sometimes felt I was sending my children mixed messages: be confident and know your inestimable worth, but also be humble and resist the temptations of pride.

Over the years, another challenge surfaced: a tension between having confidence in my Christian faith and having humility about

1. For just a few examples from recent literature extolling humility for the modern world, see Dickson, *Humilitas*; Hess and Ludwig, *Humility Is the New Smart*; D. Collins et al., *Joy of Humility*; Foster, *Learning Humility*; Edwards, *Humility Illuminated*.

my beliefs. This struggle had started early, since many of my neighborhood friends as a child were practicing Muslims. Even then, I wondered: Does being humble about my Christian faith mean acknowledging that they might be right and I might be wrong, about the entire direction of my belief and living? As I grew up, I found that this tangle of questions often made it hard to have serious gospel conversations and left me wondering how to have both humble and confident faith.

So perhaps it should be no surprise that when I was in graduate school and had the chance to do some independent research, I chose to focus on the concept of humility. There I confirmed three hunches. First, humility really is inescapably central to the Christian faith, receiving key attention in Scripture and becoming known as the hallmark of Christian ethics in the earliest centuries of Christianity. Second, the concept of humility had taken some serious hits in the Enlightenment era, as Western societies were rethinking their ethical systems from the ground up, often without the aid of religion and revelation. And third: In part because of that history, a tangle of misunderstandings often prevents us from thinking clearly about humility today.

I devoted the next few years of my life to trying to get a better handle on these discussions, trying to discern how the Bible and early Christian thinkers could help us gain a better sense of what humility is and how to cultivate it authentically.[2] This book is an attempt to share some of what I learned about this trait that stands at the center of any Christian's attempt to follow faithfully after Jesus. I hope to demonstrate that a Christian vision of humility is at the very core of the good news. In fact, it may be the most powerful and revolutionary trait that Christianity has brought to the world; getting a clear understanding of humility and making it central to our lives is in many ways the definitive quest of the Christian life.

2. For the scholarly work that underlies this book, see Pardue, "Humility"; Pardue, "Kenosis and Its Discontents"; Pardue, *Mind of Christ*; and Porter et al., "Religious Perspectives on Humility."

PLAN OF THE BOOK

The book will take us on the first steps of that quest in six chapters. Our starting point in chapter 1 is a serious consideration of humility's detractors. More than any other Christian virtue, humility has come in for serious critique across the ages. Early Christians took an enormous risk by advocating for humility in a cultural context that highly prized muscular confidence and self-promotion over modesty or self-sacrifice. Leading lights of Greco-Roman culture regarded humility as a vice that must be constrained, especially in those tasked with leadership. We face something similar in the modern era, in which humility has been criticized as a tool for manipulation of others—a way to get the weak to submit and to prevent critical thinking. While we will focus in this first chapter on what these arguments get wrong, we will also see that they get some things right. It is true that making humility central in our communities can be a risky business, and we must be alive to those risks from the start of our journey.

A principal way to avoid these pitfalls is to ensure that our view of humility is shaped by the Bible and the gospel, rather than by common counterfeit versions of the virtue that will lead us astray. To this end, chapter 2 sketches a definition of humility rooted in close reading of Scripture alongside early Christian thinkers. In Scripture we learn of a humility that is central to our identity as finite and fallen creatures. We also learn humility when we recall that we come from the dust (in Latin *humus*, from which we get the word "humility"). Yet the good news is that humility connects us not only to our earthy origins but also to our Creator—a God who is in the habit of remarkable acts of humility designed to draw us into perfect fellowship with him.

The rest of the book applies this Christian vision of humility to three areas of modern life in which humility raises new questions and holds unexpected power. Chapter 3 focuses on the puzzling and sometimes tense relationship between self-esteem and humility. Christians have a complex relationship with self-worth. On the one hand, we affirm that every human is an image bearer of infinite worth, capable of reflecting the divine image unlike any other creature. And so we have, in a way, the highest possible view of humanity.

On the other hand, we believe that a central element—arguably *the* central element—of living out the gospel is to accept our status as sinners who fall short of our high calling, throwing ourselves at the feet of Jesus in full surrender and allegiance. All of this often leaves us conflicted about how to honor our worth and the worth of others without becoming proud, and how to be humble without regarding ourselves as mere worms. We'll look carefully at this tangled mess and see how the gospel can guide us forward.

Chapter 4 tackles another area where humility and confidence often seem to be in tension: religious conviction. In the twenty-first century, most people live and work alongside neighbors from various faith backgrounds, and there is a consensus that a key element of being a good citizen, neighbor, or friend is to be humble about our beliefs about God and morality. In some ways, it is deeply Christian to hold our personal convictions loosely, recognizing that God's people often get things wrong. At the same time, the New Testament calls us to a life of mission and proclamation that is possible only if we are confident in the uniqueness and efficacy of Christ's saving and revealing work. So chapter 4 will look to Scripture and the earliest Christians—who also lived in a world of profound religious plurality for help in understanding how we can interact with our non-believing neighbors in a way that reflects both humility and courage.

Chapter 5 considers how humility could be an unexpected key to helping us solve one of the most serious challenges we face in the twenty-first century: the superabundance of information now available to us. The vast acceleration in the development and availability of knowledge has been a defining feature of human progress in recent years. Yet rather than making us happier and wiser, this multiplication of knowledge has often left us paralyzed, puzzling over how to make sense of all the competing claims on our attention. In this chapter, we will see that previous generations of Christians faced similar dynamics and viewed it as a fundamental matter of Christian discipleship. We'll learn from how they applied humility as a principal element in directing our curiosity toward the goals of wisdom and friendship with God.

Finally, a concluding chapter draws together the key insights of the book and offers a summary of the practical guidance offered by early and medieval Christian thinkers regarding how best to cultivate humility. Our forebears in the faith recognized that like a prized gem, humility can be obtained only at great personal cost and with intentional, persistent effort carried out under God's gracious provision. Long before the self-help movement emerged, they created programs of study and practice designed to help Christians cultivate humility. These practices remain relevant today, even if their particulars often need adjustment to be contextualized into modern life.

GETTING THE MOST OUT OF THIS BOOK

A few years ago, I came to recognize I needed to change my approach to physical health. As much as I was enjoying it, I recognized it would be irresponsible as an aging father of four to maintain the atrocious diet and sedentary lifestyle of my youth. So I made some changes to my eating, started running regularly, and joined a gym.

In the process, I learned that the path to fitness was trickier than I had anticipated. I discovered that when I tried to tackle unrealistic goals in my running, I not only failed to meet them but wound up discouraged enough that I would avoid running again for days or weeks. I also learned that it was easy to get injured when learning to lift weights for the first time, especially if you are too self-conscious to ask others for help. Slowly, I began to understand that without the right motivations, expectations, and support mechanisms, my attempts to get healthier could lead me in exactly the wrong direction.

After years of studying how Christians throughout history have thought about and pursued humility, I have learned that there is a similar dynamic at work here: if we aren't careful, our efforts to cultivate humility can quickly become a vexing and even counterproductive endeavor. In the interest of helping us avoid these errors, I recommend three practices as we get started.

1. Read and think about humility with others.

First, I would encourage you to process what you are reading and learning alongside others. One of the great challenges in learning about humility is that, more than most virtues, it's deeply connected not only to what we do but to how we think and feel. So trying to grow your humility muscles will require a certain degree of introspection.

But going on this journey alone can be risky. For some, this process of self-examination can lead to a crippling level of self-criticism as they discover deeper and deeper levels of pride that they didn't realize were there before. Others may experience something quite different: as they learn about humility and pride, they will tend to see examples of pride all around them and will see themselves as similar to the persecuted and lowly example of Jesus. Though they may keep these observations to themselves (knowing that they will sound proud if they voice them!), their internal life will not be transformed by the gospel but will instead atrophy into an ugly kind of martyr complex. Most will be somewhere between these two realities, perhaps riding a "humility-pride roller coaster" from day to day.

The most effective strategy for not getting lost in your own self-reflection as you try to cultivate humility is to open up to others along the way. When we are authentic and open with trustworthy companions, we are more prone to recognize our exaggerated or extreme self-analyses. In addition, a trusted companion can help us spot the areas where pride may be hiding unrecognized or where our humility may be developing in unhealthy directions.

2. Be self-aware as you consider how to apply what you learn.

Having others alongside you as you work to cultivate humility will also help with a second recommendation: being self-aware as you apply what you learn. More than most virtues, a person's growth in humility may look quite different depending on who they are and where they are starting from.

Consider, for example, how the journeys toward humility for two imaginary people—Sam and Anna—might look different. Sam is the founder and CEO of a successful business who is well loved and highly regarded by just about everyone he knows. He is often invited into leadership roles in his community and his church. Meanwhile, Anna works as a custodian at Sam's business, and she is not so much despised by the white-collar workers around her all day as she is not regarded at all. She is relatively poor, and because she has moved far away from her family for work, she also has a relatively small social network. Most days, she is physically exhausted from eight or more hours of manual labor.

Christians across the ages have affirmed that both Sam and Anna can and should benefit from cultivating humility, and to some degree this process will look similar for the two of them. After all, every person—whether poor or rich, powerful or marginalized, male or female—needs the healing power of Christ-shaped humility. But in important ways, what humility requires of Sam and Anna, and even the concrete effect it will have on their lives, will be incredibly different. As we will see in chapter 1, critics of humility over the years have rightly pointed out that humility can easily become a way for the socially powerful to keep marginalized people at bay, encouraging them to accept their lowly status and not to question or fight against injustice, while the powerful are permitted simply to mouth humble platitudes.

We will discuss later some specific ways that a Christian account of humility has some built-in safeguards against these dangers. But here at the start of our journey, I would encourage you simply to take stock of where you are located. Be careful not to oversimplify here; being relatively wealthy or well connected does not automatically mean you are proud any more than being poor and isolated is a fail-safe against pride. In addition, we should remember that these are subjective rather than objective measures, and our fallen nature causes most of us to underestimate how generously we have been blessed and overestimate the gifts God has given others. But doing our best to be self-aware as we start the process of cultivating humility is crucial if we are to make the most of what the gospel has to say to us in our individual contexts and locations.

3. Focus on how humility can transform your life with God.

The final recommendation I have is this: resist the urge to make your journey toward humility about mere "self-improvement."

This advice cuts a bit against the grain of the current moment. In the last twenty years or so, humility has developed a remarkable track record, as study after study demonstrates that the virtue is correlated with all kinds of desirable outcomes. Scholars of business strategy highlight it as a keystone for excellent leadership,[3] and psychologists have documented humility's correlation with a slew of positive character traits such as generosity,[4] openness to asking for and offering forgiveness,[5] cooperativeness,[6] and overall life satisfaction.[7] This is just the tip of the iceberg of scholarship showing that humility has all kinds of valuable effects for those who cultivate it. In my research for this book, I got a laugh when I discovered an article entitled "How Humility Will Make You the Greatest Person Ever."[8]

It is true that Scripture often promotes pursuing a life of virtue in part because of the benefits it confers on those who cultivate

3. J. Collins, "Level 5 Leadership."
4. Exline and Hill, "Humility."
5. Shepherd and Belicki, "Trait Forgiveness."
6. Hilbig and Zettler, "Pillars of Cooperation."
7. Krause, "Wisdom, Humility, Life Satisfaction."
8. Zakrzewski, "How Humility Will Make."

them. A primary theme in Proverbs, for example, is that cultivating the fear of the Lord helps us live longer, wiser, and more honorable lives. In Prov 15:33, this concept is even linked with humility: "The fear of the LORD," we read, "is instruction in wisdom, and humility comes before honor." A saying near the end of the book is even more straightforward about the reward of humility: "One's pride will bring him low, but he who is lowly in spirit will obtain honor" (Prov 29:23). Jesus echoes the sentiment of this saying, explaining to his disciples that "the greatest among you shall be your servant. Whoever exalts himself will be humbled, and whoever humbles himself will be exalted" (Matt 23:11–12).

So Scripture clearly commends humility in part by informing us of its benefits. Yet most of us would share the intuition that there is something amiss in a person pursuing humility solely in search of honor or high status. This intuition finds expression in the joke about the man who received an award from his community recognizing him for his humility, only to have it rescinded the next week because he would not stop talking about it to everyone he met.

Christians have historically argued that we should be wary of cultivating any virtue, but especially humility, for merely instrumental reasons—that is, merely as a method for obtaining honor, success, or any created good. To work toward humility in this spirit is to get off track from the start. Such efforts rarely lead to authentic humility, driving us instead toward some false imitation of the virtue that might help us look good but ultimately causes us to wither rather than to flourish.

Augustine, one of Christianity's most astute observers of humility, was keenly aware of these risks as he observed the puzzling dynamics of humility and pride in himself as well as in those souls under his care. In his early years serving as a bishop, he answers a letter from Dioscorus, a young Christian from his own region of North Africa. Dioscorus was about to head to the big city for further education and sought guidance from Augustine about various matters of theology, and especially about how to avoid looking like a simpleton in front of his more world-wise classmates. Perhaps recognizing a bit of his younger, prouder self in the young man, Augustine makes a stunning claim to sum up his answer to Dioscorus: "So if you were to ask me, however often you might repeat the question, what are the instructions of the Christian religion, I would be disposed to answer always and only, 'Humility,' although, perchance, necessity might constrain me to speak also of other things."[9]

It should be a bit jarring to hear Augustine—the author of literally hundreds of sermons and at least a dozen major treatises about Christian theology—suggest that Christianity comes down to just this one concept. But he was not exaggerating. This is because humility is not just a virtue to be pursued as part of the journey toward becoming a good leader or cultivating better relationships with others. For Augustine, humility cultivated with these ends in mind is no humility at all but an artificial substitute in search of goods that will never satisfy.

True humility, by contrast, is the most important, recurring step we must take in our pursuit of life with the triune God: the one for whom we are made and without whom our hearts remain ever restless.[10] With that goal in mind, let's begin the process of understanding humility and how it can transform our lives as twenty-first-century followers of Jesus.

9. Augustine, *Letters* 118.3.22 (*NPNF*[1] 1:446).

10. Augustine, *Confessions* 1.1.1.

CHAPTER 1

Against Humility

Understanding the Virtue's Critics

IN AN ESSAY PUBLISHED in 1903, W. E. B. Du Bois makes a troubling observation as he describes the evolution of African-American spirituality in the 1700s:

> By the middle of the eighteenth century the black slave had sunk, with hushed murmurs, to his place at the bottom of a new economic system, and was unconsciously ripe for a new philosophy of life. Nothing suited his condition then better than the doctrines of passive submission embodied in the newly learned Christianity. Slave masters early realized this, and cheerfully aided religious propaganda within certain bounds. The long system of repression and degradation of the Negro tended to emphasize the elements of his character which made him a valuable chattel: courtesy became humility, moral strength degenerated into submission, and the exquisite native appreciation of the beautiful became an infinite capacity for dumb suffering.[1]

1. Du Bois, "Faith of Our Fathers," 199. See also the insightful discussion in Whitcomb et al., "Humility and Disparity."

With devastating clarity, Du Bois highlights for us a danger that can come along with emphasizing humility in our life together: we can easily create an environment ripe for abuse, in which those oppressing the weak or marginalized use the Christian faith as a kind of weapon against the weak. Du Bois is hardly alone. As we'll see, despite its general popularity, humility has had serious detractors for most of history, each highlighting a distinctive concern regarding the negative side effects of the virtue.

It may seem strange that this book—a meditation on the value of humility for all of life—should begin by considering the best arguments against it. But there are two reasons to consider the best arguments against humility before going any further. The first is that critics of humility, both ancient and contemporary, can help warn us against the most dangerous misunderstandings about humility. The warnings of Du Bois and others should prompt us to think carefully about what we are doing when we call our communities to humility.

Aside from this, I also see a second benefit to understanding the best arguments against humility: the process should force us to recognize that pursuing humility as a form of Christian discipleship is a costly and sometimes countercultural enterprise. Consider some of the other virtues that Christians seek to embody: courage, for example, or kindness. With very few exceptions, these are traits that are almost universally recognized as good. Whether you are a farmer in Papua New Guinea or a member of the upper class in England or a factory worker in the heart of America, your community will likely appreciate and admire you if you are a courageous and kind person. Mainstream movies and television shows almost without exception depict courage and kindness in an admirable light.

Yet humility, it turns out, is not the same kind of virtue as courage or kindness in this respect. It has a profoundly conflicted pedigree, and in today's world it is loved by some and despised by others. In many cultures and subcultures, humility is not merely thought to detract from the admiration due to a person; it is perceived as a pernicious vice, marking someone as weak or perhaps as manipulative. So if we are going to understand and aspire toward humility, our first task is to understand its fiercest opponents and to recognize the traditions and thinkers against which we are positioning ourselves. We can begin at the beginning, with the first critic of humility in recorded history.

THE DESIRE FOR GREATNESS: ARISTOTLE AGAINST HUMILITY

More than three hundred years before the birth of Jesus of Nazareth, a young man named Aristotle studied under the direction of the great teacher Plato in Athens. Aristotle was a bright student with interests spanning from biology to ethics to metaphysics, and when he became a teacher himself, he had no trouble finding employment in the courts of various aristocrats seeking his expertise. Perhaps his most significant role was acting as the personal tutor of a young man named Alexander who would go on to conquer much of the known world, eventually earning the appellation Alexander the Great.

Aristotle had a profound concern with thinking deeply about the well-lived human life, which he took to mean a life in which we as humans can obtain our most worthy ends. He argued that to live that kind of life we need a certain cluster of dispositions or traits of character—virtues—that facilitate progress toward moral excellence. Aristotle notes that what we generally consider excellences of character are usually instances of a mean between extremes. For example, we think of courage as a trait that is something between cowardice—being overly intimidated in the face of danger—and rashness—being overly eager to act without care of danger.

So far, so good, right? The problem for us comes at the end of Aristotle's list of virtues, where he describes a key trait that he calls *megalopsychia.* Sometimes translated woodenly as "great-souledness," and sometimes just as "pride," the person possessing this trait clearly has a generous sense of himself. But this is not sufficient to possess the virtue of *megalopsychia*, because Aristotle requires not only that such a person *think highly* of himself but also *be worthy of* that positive self-evaluation. The "great-souled" person, then, "thinks himself worthy of great things, being worthy of them." Those who overestimate their worth and achievements are vain, while those who underestimate their worth and achievements are *mikropsychos* or "small souled," sometimes translated as "humble."[2] Here, Aristotle seems to be drawing a direct contrast to the ideal person he has been describing, making a point of highlighting just how mistaken it would be to be praiseworthy but not to recognize it.

In fact, Aristotle goes so far as to say that it is worse to be a "small-souled" or "humble" person than it is to be vain. Both are a matter of failing to know oneself, after all, but at least a vain person harbors noble aspirations, aspiring toward greatness, even if they fail in execution and lack self-awareness. The small-souled person, by contrast, not only lacks self-awareness but fails even to aspire toward what is great, noble, and excellent. When faced with an opportunity to do something of value, he shrinks back, thinking that it is too high for him. Such a person is not only to be pitied, according to Aristotle, but is also to be despised for failing to serve society with his gifts and abilities.[3]

In our time, Aristotle has come in for plenty of criticism for his thinking along these lines. He has been accused of advocating an elitist and self-centered approach to the moral life in these paragraphs, and at some points, it's hard not to agree. The great-souled person that Aristotle describes needs nothing from anyone, even though many need help from him; he receives honors from others, though he sneers mentally that these honors still underestimate his greatness; and he hardly ever admires others, since true greatness (which he, of course, embodies) is quite rare. This is not the kind of person any of us would want as a boss, friend, or neighbor.

But perhaps Aristotle is guilty here only of uncommon honesty about the aspirations in the hearts of us all. To be sure, there is a piece of us that aspires to reach the pinnacle of our potential, whether in physical, intellectual, or moral terms. And this leads to an obvious question: If you could achieve your maximum potential in one area of life—overcoming through arduous struggle

2. Aristotle, *Nicomachean Ethics*, 65.

3. Aristotle, *Nicomachean Ethics*, 67.

your physical shortcomings, your moral foibles, or your intellectual blind spots—would it not be tragic if you were unable to recognize the magnitude of your achievement? On Aristotle's view, great-souledness is simply a combination of excellence and honest self-assessment, two things that seem generally unobjectionable on their own.

So Aristotle helps us see two problems that a healthy account of humility must consider. First, he is absolutely right in his observation that humans have an abiding desire for greatness and excellence. Even if people from different times and places may have remarkably variant visions of a well-lived life, all of us long to be in the presence of goodness, beauty, and truth, and we also yearn to reflect these things in ourselves. As Christians, we view this aspect of our humanity as the result of being crafted in the image of a God who does all things well. Like our creator, we long to bring order, beauty, and goodness into the world, including by trying to make ourselves all that we can and should be.

If this is right, and if humility is consistent with God's design for us as his image bearers, then whatever humility is, it must not require us to draw back from the pursuit of excellence. Put another way: Any understanding of humility that involves simply holding back from the pursuit of greatness must not be quite right. Thus, Aristotle helps us see that humility cannot be simply a synonym for mediocrity, and it must not require us to abandon the desire to improve and realize our potential.

Unfortunately, this is exactly how humility is sometimes understood and deployed in Christian communities. At Christian nonprofits, for example, leaders sometimes tolerate or excuse poor performance in part on the grounds that we cannot expect humble Christian workers to achieve excellence. Similarly, we can sometimes too easily settle for subpar performance in ourselves by reasoning that our finitude and fallenness prevent us from reaching higher. "I'm just made this way and can't do better." Worse still, Christian leaders may sometimes use humility as a tool to discourage those under their care from growth or study, warning that to aspire to learn too much will lead to pride. Inasmuch as he helps us see the problems with such deployments of humility, Aristotle is surely our friend.

Beyond this, there is a second area where Christians can learn from Aristotle's critique. Aristotle is right not only to warn against versions of humility that would hold us back from pursuing true greatness but also to insist that humility should not require us to mask or minimize whatever excellence we do achieve. Here we might appeal again to our status as image bearers: like our maker, who made all things good and recognized them as such, we long not only to make good things but also to celebrate them. Aside from this, we can also point to the principles of honesty and integrity. Given that God explicitly forbids deception and calls his people to truthfulness, it would make no sense if humility required us to deceive ourselves or others about our ability or performance.

Again though, the sad truth is that we often try to cultivate humility in exactly this way. When we receive a compliment for a job well done, we hem and haw and sometimes lie, minimizing our achievement outwardly, even as we inwardly recognize the greatness of our achievement. Sometimes, we may even deploy the strategy of displaying our apparent humility preemptively, precisely to get compliments in the first place. "I know that what I did is not very good," we say with our lips, when what we mean in our hearts is something like, "I hope you will tell me how good this really is!"

In his depiction of Uriah Heep, Charles Dickens helps us see this version of false humility in a way that only a great fiction writer can. Heep appears early in the plot of *David Copperfield*, proclaiming his lack of intelligence and skill, and continues to do so for much of the narrative. Yet as the events of the book unfold (spoiler alert!), we discover that Heep's "humility" has been a ruse designed to make it easier for him to manipulate his unsuspecting victims. Heep's humility was exactly the type of behavior that German philosopher Friedrich Nietzsche famously despised, leading him to argue that Christian humility was *always* a kind of manipulation, a conspiracy of the weak designed to allow them to conquer the strong through deception and false self-abasement.[4] Even if most of

4. Nietzsche, *Genealogy of Morals*, 79–80.

us are not nearly so crafty as Heep in our deployments of humility, Nietzsche and Aristotle still highlight a tension between humility and being honest about our abilities and achievements.

This tension can be eased to some degree when we adopt a fully Christian understanding of the human person. According to a biblical vision of humanity, we are creatures fundamentally dependent on both our creator and others, and this means that however great our abilities or achievements may be, we owe them at least in part to others and ultimately to God. This is the logic Paul uses, asking, "What do you have that you did not receive? And if you did receive it, why do you boast as though you did not?" (1 Cor 4:7 NIV).

This Christian principle may help us figure out how to preserve true humility even in cases where we know we are truly excellent; we will look more closely at how all this works in the next chapter. But even if the tension can be mitigated, it cannot be eliminated entirely; we must always be conscious of the challenge of being honest about our excellencies while also remaining humble.

To sum up: Aristotle helps us see two challenges with humility: first, he highlights the tension between humility and our natural human aspiration toward greatness; second, he helps us see how a desire to be (or appear) humble may lead us to deceive ourselves or others. In both cases, we can see how maintaining Christian commitments may help us manage these tensions. But we should also admit that we meet here two very real risks of pursuing humility: the deflation of our aspirations, and the matter of integrity in evaluating our excellences.

DAVID HUME AND THE "MONKISH VIRTUES"

Unfortunately, this is not where the objections to humility end. While humility became a highly regarded trait as Christianity spread around the world, another serious objector to it would arise about two thousand years after Aristotle: the Scottish philosopher David Hume (1711–76). Hume shares Aristotle's suspicion of humility but for entirely different reasons.

We can see Hume's argument against humility in a major text that broke new ground in the field of ethics. As part of the work, Hume surveys various traits that we generally regard as good and others that we generally disdain and tries to categorize each one. At the end of this investigation, he concludes that virtues are simply mental qualities that have one or more of three traits: they are either (1) *useful* for some desired end, (2) *agreeable to others*, or (3) *agreeable to ourselves*.

To illustrate what he means, he describes an imaginary character who might embody a series of positive traits that fall into these various categories. His imaginary person—Hume calls him Cleanthes—possesses the qualities of fairness and kindness, qualities that are *useful to others*. He is also wise and quick witted in analyzing, qualities that *aid himself*. Moreover, he is a natural in social situations, putting others at ease and always being at ease himself, thus being *agreeable to others*. And he possesses a deep serenity and tranquility of soul that marks him not only in his interactions with others but also when he is alone, a quality that is *agreeable to himself*.[5] Much like Aristotle's "great-souled" man, there is much to be commended here, and no doubt we all aspire toward these qualities. Cleanthes sounds like fun to me.

To clarify his conception of virtues further, Hume turns to the opposite sorts of qualities—traits that fail to meet any of the criteria he has proposed. Intriguingly, his first thought here is to point to humility, along with a cluster of other traits and practices that often come together in the Christian tradition. Hume writes that "celibacy, fasting, penance, mortification, self-denial, *humility*, silence, solitude, and the whole train of monkish virtues" are rightly rejected "by men of sense" everywhere, precisely because they fail to meet these basic tests.[6] Rather than aiding us or others, these practices "stupify the understanding and harden the heart, obscure the fancy and sour the temper."[7]

5. Hume, *Enquiry*, 107–8.

6. Hume, *Enquiry*, 108; emphasis added.

7. Hume, *Enquiry*, 108.

In other words, Hume argues that these traits—even if they are highly regarded by the Christian clergy—ultimately work at cross-purposes to our typical aims as humans, making us less useful and less agreeable to others and ourselves. As a result, like Aristotle (though he seems to have come to his conclusion independently), Hume considers humility to be a vice rather than a virtue.[8]

What should we make of Hume's argument? As with Aristotle, we may first quibble with elements in Hume's theory of what makes a virtue. Most theists would think that how a trait aligns or does not align with God's demands on his creatures, for example, is worth considering when evaluating virtues and vices, and Hume leaves such matters entirely out of his calculations. Aside from this, even nontheists could (and have) wondered about Hume's assumption that self-denial, silence, solitude, or humility do not make people more agreeable and useful. Psychologists have demonstrated, for example, that people tend to prefer leaders who bear the marks of humility, and business leaders have also highlighted the value of this trait for economic success.

Nevertheless, there is something to learn from Hume's critique, even if he exaggerates about the uselessness of humility. At the very least, we can acknowledge that he is no doubt correct that people steeped in solitude, self-denial, humility may not be the life of a party. Yet a more serious accusation likely underlies Hume's sentiments here. Elsewhere, Hume is deeply critical of what may be broadly labeled asceticism—customs and ways of life that are oriented around self-denial, sometimes in extreme forms. Consider, for example, the practice of self-flagellation, in which some Christians literally whip themselves to the point of drawing blood in order to identify more closely with the self-denial of Christ. Where I live in the Philippines, there is a long tradition in which devout individuals will have themselves crucified for up to an hour (nails in the palms and all), partly to cultivate the kind of self-denying humility that Jesus demonstrated. After all, what could be a more precise imitation of Christ?

8. For an insightful consideration of Hume alongside other modern thinkers, see Bellitto, *Humility*, 96–133.

These examples may seem far-fetched, but they merely serve to highlight in the extreme a difficulty that is more pervasive in weaker forms. Countless Christians have been influenced by the notion that imitating Christ's humility requires certain kinds of self-denial that are ostensibly harmful and life denying, whether those practices involve self-inflicted pain, self-hatred, or deep self-abasement. These trends are most notable in monastic contexts; consider, for example, the admonition in a section focused on the cultivation of humility in the widely used *Rule of St. Benedict*: "Whether he sits, walks, or stands, his head must be bowed and his eyes cast down. Judging himself always guilty on account of his sins, he should consider that he is already at the fearful judgment."[9] Almost a millennium later, Thomas à Kempis's bestseller *The Imitation of Christ* would open his advice to Christians this way: "Truly to know and despise self is the best and most perfect counsel. To think of oneself as nothing, and always to think well and highly of others is the best and most perfect wisdom."[10]

You might have never been around Christians who try to live by Benedict's or Thomas's exhortations to sullenness. But you have likely been around Christians who have adopted martyr-like conceptions of their lives, considering it their duty to resist the temptation to have too much fun. Every Christian subculture does this a bit differently. In some communities, Christians highlight their frugality or poverty as a way of demonstrating their humble way of life. In others, we lament our busy schedules with faux modesty, which not only shows others our importance but also highlights a kind of modern-day "suffering." And sometimes, Christians just refuse to participate in fun activities, thinking that this is, in itself, a way of cultivating the humility of their savior.

So even if Hume is not entirely right, we can learn from his objection. Whatever our vision of Christian humility is, it must not be that as we grow in humility we become, as Hume might say, more useless and disagreeable people. Instead, we should seek a vision of humility that is compatible with a joyful and even winsome

9. Benedict, *Rule*, 20.

10. Kempis, *Imitation of Christ*, 3.

way of life, offering the world a picture of the goodness available in fellowship with the triune God.

HUMILITY AMONG THE MARGINALIZED: MARY WOLLSTONECRAFT

If Hume helps us see that certain versions of humility can be bad for all people, we must now also face a more serious concern: that the adverse effects of humility run amok are especially serious for the oppressed and downtrodden, many of whom have had the virtue of humility used for their disempowerment and manipulation. One of the first thinkers to highlight this reality was Mary Wollstonecraft (1759–97), a British author who is now best known for writing *A Vindication of the Rights of Woman*, a treatise defending gender equality. Wollstonecraft lived a tragically short and tumultuous life, having her inheritance squandered by her father before she came of age and experiencing a series of tragic relationships in her adult life.

In her exploration of what social equality between the sexes may mean, Wollstonecraft devotes an entire chapter to modesty and humility, traits that were taken at the time to be especially appropriate for women. Wollstonecraft wastes no time in noting that the embodiment of these traits has often led women to assume an unduly passive role in society. She initially seeks to distinguish what she takes to be authentic modesty—"that soberness of mind which teaches a man not to think more highly of himself than he ought to think"—and more problematic traits that are closely related.[11] Among these, humility comes in for particularly acerbic treatment.

Wollstonecraft's concern with humility is, in a way, a combination of the complaints lodged by Aristotle and Hume. Like Aristotle, she despises the humble person's tendency to see an opportunity for true greatness but to shrink back, thinking herself unworthy of it. She points to George Washington, who at the time of her writing had only recently helped make the American

11. Wollstonecraft, *Vindication*, 198.

Revolution a military success, and suggests that it is in precisely such situations that one wants a leader who is *not* humble. "Had he been merely humble," she avers, "he would probably have shrunk back irresolute, afraid of trusting to himself the direction of an enterprise, on which so much depended."[12] Thus, Wollstonecraft shares with Aristotle a concern that proper human greatness is fundamentally incompatible with humility.

But this is not all. Wollstonecraft also shares with Hume a frustration with humility's tendency to make people, and women in particular, timid, passive, and self-demeaning. At the time, social norms often required such self-abasement on the part of women, so that even in situations where they knew a subject better than their husbands, for example, they were encouraged to hold their tongues to preserve the male ego. Worse still, Wollstonecraft notes, exhortations to passivity grounded in modesty or humility generally function to keep women in harmful, even abusive circumstances. In this way, Wollstonecraft echoes Hume's concern that humility functions, unlike most positive moral traits, to decrease one's utility and agreeability.

Wollstonecraft regards humility as dangerous not merely for individuals but also for societies. Wollstonecraft lived through both the American and French Revolutions, movements that were characterized by a boldness of vision that can hardly be characterized as humble, and yet most of us would regard the results of these struggles quite positively. Wollstonecraft, who was enamored enough of the French Revolution that she moved to Paris in the middle of it, even in the face of no small danger, makes an important and convincing point in this regard. If we want only humble citizens and leaders, then we can kiss such movements goodbye. And this is, in the end, not only to the detriment of all of society; it is particularly harmful to those who have been pushed to society's edges. The poor, the downtrodden, and the marginalized are likely to stay that way, we might argue, if humility is the primary social virtue.[13]

12. Wollstonecraft, *Vindication*, 198.

13. For a real-world example, consider how colonial governments often

There is a ring of realism to some of Wollstonecraft's arguments. Tragically, what often allows abusive treatment to fester in Christian homes or churches is victims' willingness to accept their mistreatment as a matter of humble submission. After all, Jesus did not answer his accusers but accepted the shame of the cross like a lamb being led to the slaughter; so should his followers not also accept suffering without complaint or objection? Especially if one is on the margins of society and without much self-confidence, it is certainly not hard to draw the conclusion that humility demands a similar kind of passivity of Christians experiencing unjust treatment today.

This is perhaps the most poignant challenge for a serious account of humility today: to articulate a view of the virtue that will not leave the most vulnerable among us even worse off than they were before. Unlike Aristotle's and Hume's objections, this concern has special resonance for *Christian* accounts of humility, precisely because we seek to emulate a crucified Lord, and we exalt a God who is depicted in Scripture as a slain lamb.

It is also the case that the history of Christianity offers some counterarguments to Wollstonecraft's concerns. For example, early Christians often suffered, but not quietly, and even invoked the example of Christ in the process.[14] For most of Christian history, the faith has had more appeal among the outcasts and downtrodden than in any other sectors of society, and most of its adherents would suggest that their faith is a generally empowering force in their lives. Often, it is the very humility and suffering of Jesus that is so comforting and empowering to believers in such circumstances. In some paradoxical way, Jesus's example of divine humility furnishes his downtrodden followers with a grammar for interpreting their suffering in ennobling terms.[15] And so, a sufficiently Christian

relied as much on the Christian call to humility as on military might in order to prevent subjugated peoples from rebelling (Rieger, *Christ and Empire*, 43–54).

14. For example, in the Martyrdom of Polycarp, an elder in the church goes to his execution willingly but not without resistance and arguments in his defense. Paul also defended himself while being persecuted, especially by pointing out that his status as a Roman citizen afforded him certain privileges.

15. Edwards, *Humility Illuminated*, 155–71.

approach to this virtue will require taking seriously both those who see Jesus's model of humility as fundamentally disempowering *and* those who see it as a liberating, ennobling trait.

CONCLUSION

I don't take any of these objections to be mere "straw men," deserving only flippant responses. Instead, all three arguments speak to real concerns that we must keep in mind as we seek to articulate how humility should shape Christian discipleship. To sum up, the objections boil down this way: (1) humility is fundamentally at odds with our desire for and achievement of greatness; it requires either that we refuse to aspire to great things or that we deceive ourselves and others when we do achieve greatness; (2) humility can lead (and often has led) people to deny good and important aspects of being human, making us less useful and enjoyable people to our families, friends, and colleagues; and (3) humility can function merely to reinforce the status quo, even in acting as an accomplice in the abuse of those who are marginalized.

To be clear, I do not take any of these flaws to be fatal to the classically Christian conception of humility; otherwise this would be a short book indeed! But I do think a sufficient grasp of these critiques of humility is fundamental to crafting a stronger, more vibrant vision of the virtue. At their best, these objections can point us away from the counterfeits of humility and toward a genuinely Christian view of discipleship in which humility takes its cues from God's self-revelation in the Law, the Prophets, and in these last days, his Son (Heb 1:2). That task will be the burden of the rest of the book. But as we close this survey of humility's detractors, I want to make one general point about the path forward that I will be recommending.

Savvy readers will have noted that each objection in this chapter acquires its weight at least in part from its connection to the teaching, life, and death of this Jesus. That is, Aristotle, David Hume, and Mary Wollstonecraft each present problems with humility that are especially poignant for Christians because we venerate a person who literally lets himself be unjustly crucified without objection and who promotes a radical kind of self-demotion. Given this connection, you may think that the ideal strategy for escaping these theological and ethical knots would be to *de-emphasize* the ways in which Jesus is our paradigm for life. There is some wisdom here; while we are called to walk in the footsteps of Jesus, this does not entail literally imitating every aspect of his life, which was characterized by a particular mission and calling.

But in this book, I will argue that our primary failure as Christians has been precisely the opposite one—a failure to take Jesus seriously enough in our understanding of humility. That is, I believe we have generally accepted accounts of humility that are simply not Christological or even Christian enough, and this has happened in such subtle and complicated ways that our failure has been difficult to recognize.

I hope to show that it is in the person and work of Christ—rightly understood as the culmination of all of God's redemptive plan—that we witness a kind of humility that is complementary to, rather than in conflict with, greatness and excellence. In Jesus, we see a revelation of what it is to be fully human, rather than a denial of life and its various goods. In Jesus, we see no prohibition on revolutionary thinking but rather a shocking willingness to upturn the status quo without fear and to uplift the downtrodden and marginalized in the process.

This is not to say that the answer to these objections is simple or simplistic. No aspect of Christian discipleship should be. But it does suggest that a way forward is possible and that the path ineluctably leads us to a feeding trough in Bethlehem, to bloodied wooden beams on a hill outside of Jerusalem, and ultimately to a resurrected and reigning, but scarred, Lord. We know where our account of humility must end, then. What's left is to find our way there through the pages of Scripture and the wisdom of our Christian forebears.

CHAPTER 2

The God Who Swings Low

How Christ-Shaped Humility Changes Everything

The life of Athanasius, a bishop serving in the key city of Alexandria for much of his adult life, sometimes looks like a screenplay for a contemporary thriller. Multiple times he was thrown out of Alexandria by angry mobs and then welcomed back by equally large crowds after a brief exile, and he was constantly engaged in theological debates that were laced with political intrigue. In the fourth century, theological debate was a contact sport, and one in which the masses were heavily invested.

At the time, there was fierce conflict about the precise nature of Jesus's relationship to God the Father, and Athanasius preached and wrote a great deal about this subject, arguing that if Jesus of Nazareth wasn't God himself in the flesh, our faith is worthless. Those who argued against him had complicated reasons for doing so, but a key aspect of their argument was this: the Bible depicts God as a high and exalted being, unlimited in his power and knowledge, and without beginning or death. Since Jesus of Nazareth seemed to be, in fact, the antithesis of many of those things, he could be, at best, only a holy and excellent creature.

In the middle of this explosive debate, Athanasius wrote a short but influential book in which he tried to describe what we know about the deep mystery of God's becoming flesh. He argues that the incarnation is the supreme case of God descending and condescending in order to reach his creatures, who had been hopelessly exiled from him because of their fall into sin. He is careful to note that while the incarnation is unquestionably unique among all of God's acts, it is not an uncharacteristic move.

In fact, we can see that even from the first moment of creation, the author of the universe is disposed to descend to his creatures to ensure their flourishing. Genesis records the special way in which he stoops low for the benefit of humans in particular, giving them his own divine breath (Gen 2:7) and stamping on their hearts the divine image (1:26–27). By no merit of his own, Abraham and his descendants are the target of God's special condescension (Gen 12), such that in the tabernacle and then the temple, the triune God—who needs no community to enjoy eternal bliss—comes to dwell with his people (Ezek 37:18–28). Over and over, he bends low by communicating through the prophets, choosing to reveal his infinite nature through the finite channel of human language spoken by limited human messengers.

For Athanasius, the main point of this biblical survey of God's ways is to demonstrate the fundamental continuity between the incarnation and God's previous redeeming work. But his argument also has an added benefit for us: as he traces God's long-term strategy of redemption by "swinging low," he also offers the skeleton of what we might call a "biblical theology of humility." In other words, he gestures at a way of understanding "humility" that is particularly rooted in the Christian story of creation, fall, and redemption that unfolds on the pages of Scripture.

We saw in the previous chapter that cultivating the wrong kind of humility can have devastating effects. Rather than leading to human flourishing and the exaltation of the lowly, a misshapen vision of humility will hold us back, make us miserable, and create conditions where the weak can be oppressed. If this is right, then before we can talk responsibly about cultivating humility in our lives, our first step must be to ensure that we understand what humility is.

As Athanasius discovered sixteen hundred years ago, the Bible offers the key ingredients for a Christian view of humility, since it shows us how humility is fundamentally interwoven with every element in the biblical story. It is critical to understanding humans' place in the universe that God created, both before and after the fall into sin; it shapes the way in which Israel is redeemed from the land of Egypt and prescribes its national character in and out of exile; and it is a critical element in the redeeming love of Jesus of Nazareth. Only when we look at this whole picture can we grasp the biblical vision of humility.

In this chapter, we'll trace that trajectory carefully. This will take some time, but in the end, we'll have a clear, biblically informed sense of what humility is, and as a result, we'll be ready to figure out how to make it central to our lives as we seek to follow Jesus. Let's begin by thinking about how the biblical teaching on creation shapes our grasp of the elusive virtue.

HUMILITY AND CREATION

We humans have a history of placing ourselves at the center of things. The Copernican Revolution in the sixteenth century was at first deeply unpopular because, among other things, it seemed like a demotion for humanity to suggest that our planet is not the privileged center of the universe. And even if modern people know that the universe doesn't revolve around them, we still interpret all kinds of other natural phenomena through the lens of our own humanity. A case in point is the way we tend to treat animals, especially pets, as little more than smaller, furrier human beings, projecting our desires and interests onto them, and even sometimes (disturbingly, in my own view) dressing them like us. Of course, our pets are no more humanoid in their desires and appetites than the earth is the center of the universe, but we don't typically let that stop us.

This anthropocentrism is an understandable if regrettable feature of the human condition. After all, we are incredible creatures, capable of remarkable things in comparison to the rest of the animal kingdom. The psalms often comment on the remarkable capability and intricacy of the human creature. We are "fearfully and wonderfully made" (Ps 139:14), and the Lord has seen fit to set his creation under our authority, crowning us with glory and honor (8:5–8). The story of Adam and Eve has clear royal overtones, so that their significance is not only their status as our first parents but also as the king and queen of Yahweh's good earth, entrusted to bring order and governance to the world.

But in the same breath that the psalmist describes humanity's exalted place in God's *cosmos*, he also highlights another critical feature of our species. In the scope of the universe, we are almost hilariously small. "When I look at your heavens, the work of your fingers," the psalmist comments in Ps 8:3–4, "What is man that you are mindful of him, and the son of man that you care for him?" By invoking the awe and wonder that every human has felt when examining the scope of the universe, the psalmist aims simultaneously to highlight what a promotion humanity received in the garden but also how unearned that promotion was. To underscore this point further, he likens Yahweh's salvation to working through "babies and infants" (v. 2) to achieve military victory. The point here is not to suggest that humanity is merely a puppet for achieving divine ends or a pawn in a cosmic game of chess but that we should not overestimate the degree to which we deserve the special privileges that we enjoy as the governors of creation and the focal point of God's redemptive plan.

Humanity's smallness in view of God and his creation is a consistent theme in the Old Testament, and it is perhaps nowhere better expressed than in Job 38–41. In the preceding chapters, the righteous Job has lost everything, and due in part to the needling of his friends, he finally questions the justice of his plight before God. Then, after having been silent for most of the book, God finally breaks his silence. In a four-chapter speech, God appeals, like the psalmist, to the vastness and complexity of the created order, highlighting how much of it Job (or humanity generally) can neither understand nor master.

To his credit, Job understands exactly the point of God's argument, responding by saying simply, "Behold, I am of small account; what shall I answer you? I lay my hand on my mouth. I have spoken once, and I will not answer; twice, but I will proceed no further" (Job 40:4–5). While the word "humility" is never used here, it's clearly at stake in Job's response to God. In Yahweh's speech, vocabulary associated with pride is used multiple times, and large swaths of the monologue are designed to highlight how minor most sources of human pride—especially technology and mastery of nature—actually are.

This theme recurs frequently throughout the Old Testament, as the biblical authors try to help us recognize and embrace our lowliness in the scope of the created order. The psalmist writes, "Though the Lord is high, he regards the lowly, but the haughty he knows from afar" (Ps 138:6). Similarly, we are told that while God opposes scornful hearts, "to the humble he gives favor" (Prov 3:34); we learn that out of the whole created order, Yahweh has special concern for those who are "humble and contrite in spirit" (Isa 66:2). The prophets are fond of noting that blessing from Yahweh is available only to those who humble themselves, both individually—"Seek humility; perhaps you may be hidden on the day of the anger of the Lord" (Zeph 2:3)—and corporately—"If my people who are called by my name humble themselves . . . then I will hear from heaven and will forgive their sin and heal their land" (2 Chr 7:14).

Throughout the Old Testament, then, we have a clear general principle being expressed: while pride brings a person low, God exalts those who are lowly in spirit. One of the most interesting places where the Old Testament takes us in this regard has to do with Yahweh's concern for the poor. The vocabulary that the Old Testament uses for poverty and humility is clearly overlapping, something that is still evident in English: when we talk about someone having a "humble" way of life, we mean something about their economic status. This overlap helps us make sense of the different ways in which Matthew and Luke render one part of Jesus's Sermon on the Mount: where Matthew records, "Blessed are the poor in spirit" (Matt 5:3), a concept in the neighborhood of humility to be sure, Luke records simply, "Blessed are you who are poor" (Luke 6:20).[1]

It would be a mistake to think that these overlapping concepts—humility and poverty—are identical with one another. In Hebrew and in Greek (as in English), there are still clear ways of differentiating humility from economic poverty. But in both the Old and New Testaments, the idea seems to be that while economic hardship is not necessarily a prerequisite for cultivating humility, poverty tends to move us in the general direction of humility.[2]

But for now, the key thing to note is that Scripture describes humility, at least in part, as *a tendency to look past the great accomplishments of our hands, or of our nation, or even our species, and to see the smallness and lowliness that is actually our reality.* When we embrace that reality, the Bible clearly teaches, we are positioning ourselves for being lifted up. Perhaps the most potent expression of this principle occurs in the Gospel of John, where Jesus consistently speaks about his being "lifted up" when describing his impending death on the cross (e.g., John 3:14; 8:28; 12:32). Here, we see the ultimate expression of the general truth that God exalts the lowly.

HUMILITY AND THE FALL INTO SIN

But we are getting ahead of ourselves by speaking of Christ's redeeming work. We noted earlier that humility plays a key role in every aspect of Scripture's narrative, and between creation, which we have just treated, and redemption, which we will treat next, there is a major piece of the biblical narrative missing: sin. The way Scripture tells it, humility requires that we recognize not only our small role in creation but also the depths to which we have sunk in our entanglement with sinful habits and systems.

1. For more about this distinction, see Bock, *Luke*, 1:931–44.
2. See further Edwards, *Humility Illuminated*, 159–62.

Have you ever wondered why we describe the first sin of Adam and Eve as "the fall"? Rather than simply using language of "going astray" or "missing the mark," both of which are also fine metaphors for sin, we tend to favor a spatial image of descent when talking about the first transgression. This language, as far as I can tell, is never used in Scripture to describe Adam and Eve's sin, but for at least a millennium this concept has been the chief way that Christians across diverse languages and cultures have chosen to describe what happened to humanity in the garden. Though it's difficult to trace the origins of this concept, one passage that has likely shaped this way of speaking is Isa 14:12–14:

> How you are fallen from heaven, O Day Star, son of Dawn! How you are cut down to the ground, you who laid the nations low! You said in your heart, "I will ascend to heaven; above the stars of God I will set my throne on high; I will sit on the mount of assembly in the far reaches of the north; I will ascend above the heights of the clouds; I will make myself like the Most High."

You might have heard of this passage as a description of Satan's transformation from an archangel to God's archenemy. People often draw a line between this text and Rev 12:3–4 and argue that what is being described here is a primordial fall in the spiritual realm, in which Lucifer, an angel of the Lord, takes one-third of the angels with him in rebellion against God.

Modern commentators have noted that there are problems with this mode of interpretation. The text itself is clearly nestled in a section decrying the arrogance and wickedness of the king of Babylon, and it is this actual, historical person whom Israel seems to be taunting in the context. While there is clearly a parallel between the king's prideful, oppressive stance and the intentions and attitude of Satan, we have no indication from the text itself that a shift in subject has occurred.

Nevertheless, I don't think we have to abandon altogether the notion that what is described in Isa 14 is typologically descriptive of sin and even of the first sin. In fact, Scripture repeatedly describes the result of sin as being brought low, noting the irony that sin often springs in the first place from a desire to be exalted. "One's pride will bring him low," we are told in Proverbs, "but he who is lowly in spirit will obtain honor" (Prov 29:23). This reversal of fortunes is sometimes described as a fact of life—like gravity, a result of how the universe is structured—but it is also sometimes attributed directly to divine intervention: Yahweh himself is the one who "casts the wicked to the ground" (Ps 147:6) and abases the proud (2 Sam 22:28; Ps 18:27). The book of Isaiah overflows with this imagery, as Yahweh makes it abundantly clear that he is ready to bring low both Israel and her enemies in the height of their pride (Isa 2:9–12; 5:15; 10:33; 13:11; 25:11–12; 26:5; 29:4; 32:19).

If we follow the spatial imagery of Scripture, then, it is inevitable that we will see a connection between human lowliness as a part of creation and a different kind of lowliness that is the result of sin. In other words, Scripture's depiction of the human condition requires that we consider not only our finitude—our limited role in the grand scheme of God's creation—but also our fallenness. It requires that we read Isa 14:12–14 not only as a description of some other character—the king of Babylon or Lucifer—but as a description of ourselves. We must confess that we are creatures crafted for glory and that while that splendor is still visible in glimpses, it is often obscured by sin and its diverse perversions of the human condition. Both as individuals and as communities, we have pursued a greatness buried in our souls, but in our quest to be exalted we have fallen from the heights for which we were created; we have been "humbled."

Here, we need to take our first close look at humility's opposite: pride. There is a long tradition in Christian thought of arguing that in some sense, every sin comes down to a form of pride; that ultimately, all our failures are, in some sense, arrogant attempts to be our own gods. Augustine of Hippo, a deeply influential theologian who lived in Africa in the fifth century, argued that this is both true and false. This notion is false, Augustine argues, because humans are complicated creatures, and in many situations, we do the wrong things not because we are haughty and exalted but often precisely because we live in a world so broken by sin.

Think of the victim of verbal abuse as a child, who showers his own children with the same shameful messages he received years before; or of the pregnant woman trapped in substance abuse and addiction, ignoring all her moral intuitions and obligations in order to experience a high. Those who do wrong are often not the proud but "the weeping and sorrowful."[3] In recent years, theologians have echoed and amplified this insight, noting that particularly for the marginalized, sin often springs from a lack of self-respect or even self-hatred, which is almost the opposite of arrogance. This is a worthy insight that we'll explore further in the next chapter when we talk about self-esteem.

But even as Augustine rightly dismisses the notion that every sinful act is just pride in disguise, he affirms that pride has a special place in the litany of human wrongdoing. He argues that it is pride that the serpent exploits in the garden, noting how his enticement of Adam and Eve plays on a deep desire to be equal to the Most High: "For God knows that when you eat of it your eyes will be opened, and you will be like God, knowing good and evil" (Gen 3:5). In addition to being the genesis of sin, pride also has a distinctive way of sneaking into our hearts: unlike other sins of the heart, which generally go along with external sins—envy, which leads to stealing, for example, or malice, which leads to hateful words and actions—pride tends to infect us precisely when we are doing what's right.

Moreover, pride is the most effective blocker of divine grace that we humans have at our disposal, making it a most insidious sort of disease—even as it robs us of our well-being, it tricks us into thinking that we need no medical care, sealing our fate.[4] To use a nonmedical image for a moment, pride is like Stuxnet, a computer virus famously used by an espionage team to destroy Iranian nuclear centrifuges in 2010. The malicious software had remarkable success mainly because it included a crucial and ingenious feature: it tricked computers at the nuclear facilities into showing that all

3. Augustine, *On Nature and Grace* 29.33 (*NPNF*[1] 5:132).

4. Augustine, *On Nature and Grace* 29.36 (*NPNF*[1] 5:133). See Couenhoven, "Not Every Wrong."

systems were normal, even as centrifuge after centrifuge destroyed itself. This is a perfect metaphor for the destruction brought about by pride—it can infect and destroy while also sending us the signal that we are on exactly the right track.

And so because pride has a special place in the genealogy of human sin, and because it is the most malicious and persistent virus affecting the human psyche, Augustine argues that humility is the trait without which our sinful hearts will never be cured. When we think of humility in this way, it has a different shade from what we noted earlier. We are not talking here about an acknowledgment of our smallness in the scope of the universe (the creational aspect of humility) but about a *willing admission that we have brought ourselves low through our entanglement with sin and vice.*

This is the kind of humility that is symbolized in so many rich ways in Scripture—tearing one's garments, sitting in ashes, wearing sackcloth—all of which are designed to communicate externally the internal brokenness that comes with assessing oneself with honesty. It is the narrow door through which all must enter into a life of submission and fidelity to God himself, and in this sense, humility is the gatekeeper of salvation.

HUMILITY AS THE WAY OF SALVATION

This leads us to a third way that the Christian Scriptures talk about humility. Humility involves not only accepting our finitude—our smallness in the scope of God's creation—and our fallenness—the brokenness that we inherit and then perpetuate as we aspire to the greatness for which we were created—but ultimately it involves our salvation from those things, as an infinite and perfect God descends to our rescue.

This idea is all over the New Testament, but one famous passage dominates the others in helping us see Jesus's work in terms of his humble service. In his letter to the Christians in Philippi, the apostle Paul seeks to bring the church together despite persistent divisions, and at the center of his appeal is a plea for humility. We read in Phil 2:3–11:

> Do nothing from selfish ambition or conceit, but in humility count others more significant than yourselves. Let each of you look not only to his own interests, but also to the interests of others. Have this mind among yourselves, which is yours in Christ Jesus,
>
> who, though he was in the form of God,
> did not count equality with God a thing to be grasped,
> but emptied himself,
> by taking the form of a servant, being born in the likeness of men.
> And being found in human form,
> he humbled himself by becoming obedient to the point of death,
> even death on a cross.[5]

Many biblical scholars believe that the hymn starting in v. 6 ("who, though he was in the form of God") may be the oldest piece of Christian liturgy that we have, positing that it was sung or recited in Christian churches before Paul came to use it here. Regardless of whether this hypothesis is correct, there is no question that early and modern Christians alike recognize in this song a beautiful summary of Christianity's distinctive claim: our belief in a creator who is willing to set aside his privilege and glory in order to serve and rescue his creation.

It is here that humility is vaulted from the periphery of the biblical story to its very center. When Paul wants to describe the clearest revelation of God—the incarnation of the Son in the person of Jesus of Nazareth—the trait that comes to Paul's mind is humility. What's more, Paul doesn't merely point to humility as a critical aspect of what has already been accomplished on our behalf; instead, he highlights a radical vision of humility as the enduring hallmark of Christian behavior. Both claims represent significant departures from Christianity's roots in Judaism, and both claims would have a radical impact on the church's development over the ensuing millennia.

5. Line breaks altered to illustrate poetic form.

God and Humility

Let's try to unpack these claims: first, the notion that in Christ, God reveals humility to be a fundamental aspect of his character. As we noted at the beginning of this chapter, the Christian story—that the one true God had been made incarnate as a vulnerable baby born among cattle, raised in a tiny town of no reputation, and then killed in the most ignominious way available at the time—thrust believers into an unenviable theological position. To the Jews, they had to defend the notion that the one true God who made heaven and earth and rescued Israel from Egypt in a series of mighty acts had made himself not only visible but vulnerable to death. To the Greeks, their claims seemed even more ridiculous, since most Greco-Roman intellectuals were committed to a theology that said that if there was a single divine creator, he was an impersonal being, totally separate from and uninvolved with the world of the five senses.

In this environment, however, the apostle Paul, and then later Christian thinkers like Athanasius of Alexandria and Augustine of Hippo, held tightly to the notion that divine power and divine humility were not at odds, and that surprising as it may be, the incarnation is actually in continuity with the Old Testament's description of who God is. In fact, in Phil 2 itself, scholars have argued that we have echoes of the so-called Servant Songs of Isa 40–66, which depict a messianic figure who occupies a simultaneously exalted and humbled status.[6] Isaiah 53 contains the most famous of these songs, describing the servant as one who is brought low (v. 7) but receives special recognition for his willing self-sacrifice (vv. 10–12).

Even more significantly, the early Christians pointed to the ways in which the incarnation is merely a more visible and intense revelation of God's tendency in the Old Testament to bow himself low to engage with his creatures. Think for a moment about the account of humility that we have been tracing through the biblical narrative. We have seen that it seems to have two connotations:

6. See, for example, Bauckham, *God Crucified*, 51–53.

first, it often connotes the appropriate attitude toward creaturely limits; a recognition of and submission to our finitude as created beings who represent only minor pieces of the cosmic picture (thus, Job 38–41). Second, it has to do with recognizing the descent that we have experienced because of sin; humility requires accepting that while we were created for glory, our entanglement with sin has brought us low.

The Christian claim is that every time God reveals himself or intervenes in human history to save his people, and especially in the incarnation, these two notions of humility are at work. When God speaks, for example, he always uses human language, which is a remarkably clumsy and limiting instrument for a God who is infinite and ineffable in his perfection.[7] In selecting Israel as his covenant partner and the vehicle for his saving work in the world, he does not pick the most powerful nation but allies himself with a weak and lowly set of individuals who have no special ability (Deut 7:7). Moreover, when he descends to his people through the law, the sacrificial system, and the prophets, Yahweh is not only embracing limited creaturely instruments but is also choosing to attach himself to sinful, flawed people. Though humans have brought themselves low, God meets them in the mire where they have trapped themselves.

Because of this, Christians don't see the humility revealed in Christ as a break with God's previous work but instead see it as the culminating revelation of something we already knew about God. To put it differently: While we knew before that humility had to do with *how God acted*, in Christ we find out that it is, in fact, a key aspect of *who God is*. This, it turns out, is the good news of Jesus—that God's love for us is coupled with his humility toward us; his willingness from eternity past to choose to entangle himself with our lowly estate in the most profound ways possible, for our good.

7. In addition to typical proof texts on this score (e.g., Isa 55:8–9), one of the best illustrations of this reality is the mysterious response that Yahweh offers to Moses during the burning bush encounter. Both Jewish and Christian thinkers have long struggled with the Hebrew words uttered there and have suggested (rightly, I think) that the intention is (at least in part) to highlight the gap between what human words can communicate and who God is.

Humility and the Path to Fellowship with God

But lest we get lost in the depth of the theological mysteries tied up with the matter of divine humility, we should remember that Paul's primary point in Phil 2 is not the theological truth that God is revealed in humility but that because of this truth, the Philippian Christians should cultivate humility themselves ("have this mind . . . which is yours in Christ Jesus").

This pivot from divine to human action should cause us to wonder how exactly we can follow the example of the Son of God, who laid aside *so much* authority and power to become a creature. Surely no human act, no matter how humble, could rightly be compared to that kind of condescension. Just imagine yourself, having done something that you considered particularly humble, saying to a friend or neighbor (or just yourself), "Well, now I know how the Son of God must have felt as he took on flesh and died on a cross." Not an attractive look, right?

Does Paul really think that merely human Christ followers can imitate the humility exhibited by the Son of God himself? Based on all of Paul's writings, it seems the answer here must be a resounding yes, though some caveats are in order. Repeatedly in his letters to churches, Paul urges his listeners to imitate him, even as he imitates Christ; what's more, the call to imitating Christ often centers on mimicking Jesus's humility and weakness. In 1 Cor 4:8–21, Paul is in the midst of a defense of his own ministry that focuses, at least in part, on the ways in which it echoes the ministry of Jesus. He contrasts his approach with those who are "puffed up" by their apparent knowledge or authority in the church, noting that, like Jesus, he and Apollos endure homelessness, slander, and persecution. Later in 1 Corinthians, Paul repeats the call to "be imitators of me as I imitate Christ" (11:1).

This idea of imitating God by serving others shows up consistently throughout the rest of the New Testament. In Ephesians, Paul urges his readers to "be imitators of God" (Eph 5:1), after referencing the compassion showered upon us by God in Christ (4:32). The author of Hebrews and Peter both describe discipleship as a matter of imitating Jesus and other Christians, especially in hardship (Heb 6:12; 1 Pet 2:21). Perhaps most compellingly, after Jesus washes his disciples' feet, he notes the same arc of humility evident in Phil 2—that the master becomes the servant, laying aside privilege and power in favor of the well-being of others. Then, in one of the only texts of the Gospels where Jesus is explicitly offered as an example to imitate, he calls his disciples to behave similarly toward each other.

The New Testament's Innovation: Other-Directed Humility

To sum up what we have said in this section: in the New Testament, we learn of a third dimension of biblical humility. Humility not only means embracing our creaturely limitations (our finitude) and confessing our entanglement with sin (our fallenness); it also means following after Jesus by *laying aside our rights and privileges in the interest of loving our neighbors.*

It's valuable to see that this is not an entirely novel development but that these three dimensions of humility are connected to one another. For example, in the biblical narratives, Israel and then the church are called in the Old and New Testaments to be humble—to honestly confess their creaturely limits and their sinful habits—not only because this is what will help them get right with God but *precisely so that* they can be instruments of God's love to the nations.

The connections between these three types of humility are also evident when we reflect on the practicalities of life. Becoming the kind of person who will, when appropriate, lay aside your privileges on behalf of others requires—or at least is catalyzed by—a willing embrace of your creaturely limitations as well as an acknowledgment of your entanglement with sin. Only a person who is comfortable admitting that they are not infinite can, for example, give up leadership responsibilities that need to be shared; only a person who grasps the power of sin in their life can accept that they may be on the wrong side of an argument and reconcile with their spouse.

Jesus and Paul highlight the importance of this kind of humility in their own ministry. As we have already seen, Jesus embodies this notion most clearly when he washes his disciples' feet, laying aside his privileged status as a rabbi to take care of his disciples. Paul likewise forces his audience to recognize the ways that his ministry is a matter of "swinging low." For example, he makes a point of noting that he is not in the habit of ministering with lofty speech or wisdom—which is notable because he was likely trained in the art of public speech—but "in weakness and fear and trembling," echoing the content of his message (Christ crucified) with his way of life (1 Cor 2:1–5). So both Jesus and Paul demonstrate that humility requires not merely an appropriate perspective on ourselves but an outward motion of love and service toward others.

CONCLUSION: FOLLOWING THE GOD WHO SWINGS LOW

We started this chapter by noting that we desperately need a clear, biblical picture of humility if we are going to avoid the pitfalls of cultivating a false version of the virtue, knowing that the risks involved are serious indeed. While we have by no means surveyed every biblical passage that refers to humility, we have tried to trace how humility fits into the Bible's grand narrative and found there three important aspects of humility.

First, prior to any of God's redemptive actions or special revelations, humility sets the stage for right relationship with our creator: it is that trait by which we come to recognize our limits as small parts of God's cosmic design, dependent on divine provision for food, drink, and breath. Second, we noted that humility is connected to human entanglement in sin; it involves admitting the depths to which we have sunk as creatures made for glory but gone awry. Finally, we saw that humility presses us to be other directed, laying aside our rights and using our power on behalf of others. Humility, then, is a virtue that allows us (1) to look past our great accomplishments and to see the smallness, (2) to willingly admit that we have brought ourselves low through our entanglement with sin and vice, and (3) to lay aside our rights and privileges in the interest of loving our neighbors.

Importantly, we saw that all three of these aspects of humility are revealed perfectly in Jesus of Nazareth. In his life and ministry, we see a God who embraces creaturely limits, showing us what it means to accept our identity as creatures with wisdom and obedience to God's design. Similarly, in the cross, God chooses to entangle himself with the depths of human sin, not by participating in it but by standing in solidarity with us as sinners and accepting our penalty in our place. In all of this, Jesus demonstrates for us what it means to lay aside privilege and glory to serve and ultimately save us.

I hope it's starting to become clear already how this balanced, "three-dimensional" model of humility heads off some of the objections voiced in the previous chapter. Biblical humility should not hold us back from pursuing greatness—as Aristotle feared—even if it does demand that we confront our limits as creatures. Similarly, it should not make us solemn and miserable people—as Hume argued—but should give way to honest confession of our shortcomings alongside rejoicing in God's redemptive work. And biblical, Christ-shaped humility should not result in the disempowerment of the weak and oppressed—as Wollstonecraft and Du Bois observed some versions of humility doing—because Christian communities must demand that those in power follow Jesus's example of humble service.

So far, we have remained in the realm of theory and definition. In the chapters ahead, we'll put these ideas to work and see what it means to apply this biblical, Jesus-shaped account of humility to the real problems of everyday life.

CHAPTER 3

Weighing Our Worth

Humility, Self-Esteem, and Following Jesus

CAN YOU REMEMBER THE last time you were paid a generous compliment about something important to you? Did it make you squirm a bit, unsure exactly how to reply? If so, you're not alone—as a chronic compliment deflector myself, I can verify that the internet is full of articles trying to help people like me learn how to take compliments well.

This general challenge has a special trickiness for followers of Jesus. We remember, for example, that Jesus had some strong words for people who enjoyed being praised by others for their good deeds (Matt 6:1–4), and we are all too aware of the risks that pride poses to our spiritual health. As a result, sometimes a simple, friendly interaction can turn us into anxiety-filled messes.

As early as the fourth century, we find Christians having some of the same struggles. For example, in a collection of anonymous sayings from early Christian monks who lived in the Egyptian desert in the fourth century, we read this exhortation from an older monk to those under his care: "If somebody praises you to your face, immediately reflect on your sins and entreat him in these words: 'For the sake of the Lord, brother, do not praise me for I am a wretched fellow and cannot bear it.'"[1] Aside from learning that the monks of the Egyptian desert were pretty tough on themselves and their community, this ancient saying and others like it teach us that Christians of all generations and cultural backgrounds have clearly struggled with the tension.

But our modern experience is also complicated by a key concept in contemporary psychology: *self-esteem*, the idea that acknowledging our self-worth is valuable. Since at least the 1970s, psychologists have been arguing that self-esteem is the critical missing piece for many children (and adults) who are failing in various areas of their lives. From the family to the classroom to the workplace, experts advocated approaches structured around supporting high self-regard, hoping that it would make for better families, students, and employees. It has become common in the intervening decades for not only therapists but also pastors and parents to insist that the beginning of all healing and personal growth is an ability to love yourself.

Then came the backlash. "Everybody gets a medal" was the sarcastic refrain critiquing a new world in which there were no losers and, necessarily, no winners at school and sporting events. Educators pushed back against grade inflation or in some cases the elimination of grades entirely—developments that had been driven in part by the desire to protect the high self-esteem of children who had been trained to think they were excellent at everything. And in psychology departments around the world, the pushback took a more analytical form: there has been growing academic debate about whether self-esteem is really all it's cracked up to be.

As it is with receiving compliments, this general concern about the value (or problems) with self-esteem has special importance for Christians. On the one hand, we of all people should understand the notion that humans are creatures of unique and immeasurable worth, each designed to mirror their Creator in unique and beautiful ways. Moreover, we are committed to the idea that God desires for his creatures to flourish, and if an ingredient

1. Wortley, *Sayings of Desert Fathers*, 415.

of human flourishing seems to be healthy self-esteem, we ought not despise it.

Yet we are also committed to a view of human depravity that would seem to pull in precisely the opposite direction of self-esteem; in fact, we believe that repentance and faith are possible only when we can grasp the breadth and depth of our shortcomings—when we humble ourselves. As hymn writer John Newton knew well, we can sing of God's "amazing grace" only because we know that we were once blind, lost, and wretched.[2]

In this chapter, we'll start by seeing what psychologists have learned about self-esteem and humility over the past several decades. Then we'll explore how the biblical picture—especially the story of Israel in the Old Testament and the story of Paul in the New Testament—can lead us to a new understanding of humility, self-esteem, and following Jesus. In the end, I hope that we will find that a kind of self-esteem is actually the prerequisite for authentic humility but also that humility is the only way to find stable footing for our frail human egos. And hopefully we will figure out whether the advice of that fourth-century monk is the best way to handle compliments or not.

SELF-ESTEEM: THE ORIGIN STORY

First, we should start at the beginning. The phrase "self-esteem" becomes a significant concept in psychology only a little more than a century ago. In 1890, a Harvard professor with a receding hairline and a bushy beard penned a two-volume introduction to psychology that laid much of the groundwork for the discipline as it existed for much of the twentieth century. In his groundbreaking work *The Principles of Psychology*, William James touches on everything from brain chemistry to constructs of the self to the practice of hypnosis. But what is of special interest is a small section in which James introduces into modern parlance a term that is now almost ubiquitous: self-esteem.

2. Newton, "Amazing Grace."

James explains that we all have a variety of "selves" that vie for our central desires in life. While it would be wonderful to be a world-class athlete, a philosopher, a great explorer, and a saint all at once, James explains that this is simply not possible. In reality, all of us take a look at the variety of potentialities that we may pursue, and given various factors, we select one. And it is upon that primary identity, that "self," that our aspirations hang, along with whatever embarrassment accrues to us when we are less than successful in achieving our aims.[3]

This helps explain why a world-class athlete feels disappointment when they don't win, despite being better than 99 percent of people on the planet. Watching from my couch at home, I feel no shame whatsoever that I do not corner kick like Messi, or shoot three-pointers like Steph Curry, or run like Usain Bolt. But a person whose identity has been squarely shaped in relation to the aspiration to be the very best in their sport is threatened by the prospect of even a second-place finish.

Based on this discussion, James theorizes that this thing called self-esteem can be understood in terms of a simple formula: "success divided by pretensions."[4] That is, the level of our self-esteem amounts to what we are, divided by what we hope to be. If your successes are just about equal to—or even better than—what you expected of yourself, then you're in good shape.

After proposing this formula, James goes on to explain that the key to increasing our self-esteem often comes down to reducing our hopes for ourselves, recognizing our limited time and abilities. As an example, James argues that many residents of Boston, where he resided, would be far happier if they would simply give up their aspirations to maintaining a "musical self," since they could give up the constant striving for excellence at an instrument. We experience the same kind of freedom when we are rejected by a lover, James argues—once we know for certain that we no longer

3. James, *Principles of Psychology*, 309.

4. James, *Principles of Psychology*, 310.

need to aspire to romance with a particular person, we experience a kind of release.[5]

Intriguingly, James argues in the next paragraph that this is a primary reason for the success of Evangelical Christianity at the time. The Evangelicals' robust doctrine of sin and equally powerful notion of salvation by faith alone gives us a new lease on life. Once we recognize that we are (and never will be) the saintly people we aspire to be, we no longer labor under the illusion that we must earn God's merit and can move into a place of more positive self-regard. This is a fascinating theological proposal that we will return to in due time. But first, we must trace the history of self-esteem a bit further.

For most of the twentieth century, James's concept of self-esteem would largely slumber as a concept familiar only to professional psychologists. But in the 1960s and 70s, the concept got an overhaul that led to an explosion of interest. At this point, there was a transition from thinking of self-esteem as "success divided by pretensions," into something more along the lines of the value communicated in *The Little Engine That Could*. If you can think it, dream it, imagine it—you can do it.

This idea—that "you are what you think you are" or that you are "as good as you esteem yourself to be" has become a key way of understanding the ingredients of the good life.[6] For decades, studies accumulated that seemed to make a connection between high self-regard and all kinds of success. Better educational outcomes, lower rates of criminal activity, higher income, and greater life satisfaction, to name just a few, were all shown to be correlated with high self-esteem. Given this realization, facilitated in part by the development of systems of measuring self-esteem that made it possible to study self-esteem with scientific accuracy, psychologists began focusing more and more attention on the centrality of this concept for human well-being.

In 1969, the same year of Woodstock and the first humans to walk on the moon, Nathaniel Branden brought the notion of

5. James, *Principles of Psychology*, 311.

6. Kristjánsson, *Self and Its Emotions*, 99.

self-esteem into the mainstream of American life and thought. In his book *The Psychology of Self-Esteem*, Branden argued that "there is no value-judgment more important to man—no factor more decisive in his psychological development and motivation—than the estimate he passes on himself."[7] Virtually every disorder of mental and relational health can be connected, in Branden's view, to a deficiency in a person's self-assessment of their competence and worthiness. Conversely, robust self-esteem provides us with "an inestimable weapon" against disorders of all kinds and allows us to unleash our full potential.[8]

It's hard to overstate the significance of this move, not only for professional psychologists but for wider Western culture. At every level of society, acceptance of Branden's thinking produced a special concern to cultivate and protect the self-esteem of individuals throughout society. In California, for example, a high-profile task force sought to curb criminality by offering self-esteem-boosting therapies to incarcerated individuals. Throughout the United States, approaches to discipline in schools and homes mirrored this approach, treating most offenders as if their primary problem was a deficiency in self-regard.

Yet over the years, closer analysis demonstrated that previous claims about self-esteem's effectiveness had been . . . well, greatly exaggerated. Throughout the late 1990s, study after study tried and failed to demonstrate that self-esteem could do what Branden had promised—produce high academic achievement, low rates of criminality and deviance, higher earnings, and greater occupational success. In an exacting summary and analysis of the relevant data, a prominent social psychologist, Roy Baumeister, argued in 2002 that while self-esteem may be *correlated with* these outcomes, there is good evidence that it does not cause them. Instead, the evidence suggests that causation goes the other way—that people who do well at school and work, earn a lot, and don't have criminal

7. Branden, *Psychology of Self-Esteem*, 109.

8. Branden, *Psychology of Self-Esteem*, 140.

records *happen to have* high self-esteem precisely because of all these traits.[9]

Moreover, as it turns out, it is entirely possible for bullies and violent criminals to genuinely think quite highly of themselves, and evidence suggests that simply encouraging people to think more highly of themselves will not actually do much to help them flourish. Baumeister and his coauthors' summary on this point is striking:

> We have not found evidence that boosting self-esteem (by therapeutic interventions or school programs) causes benefits. Our findings do not support continued widespread efforts to boost self-esteem in the hope that it will by itself foster improved outcomes. In view of the heterogeneity of high self-esteem [i.e., because the reasons people may have self-esteem are complex and varied], indiscriminate praise might just as easily promote narcissism, with its less desirable consequences.

In some sense, Baumeister is telling us what we all already knew: simply telling yourself that you're good, smart, and likable does not make these things so and is not likely even to help you be a healthier or happier person.

It may be tempting to take Baumeister's work as evidence squarely against the value of self-esteem. After all, it could be taken to support exactly what many Christians have argued repeatedly: that humans are naturally proud and depraved creatures who are fundamentally in need of *less* positive self-regard, not more. And of course, such an approach would fit quite neatly with many accounts of humility, in which self-esteem and humility are fundamentally at odds with one another.

But neither Scripture nor the psychological research lets us get away with such a simplistic conclusion. In terms of the psychological research, even with all the caveats, Baumeister notes that high self-esteem *does* have a very high correlation with happiness (meaning if you have one, you will probably have the other) and

9. Baumeister et al., "Does High Self-Esteem." On children in particular, an illuminating study is Smith and Elliott, *Hollow Kids.*

that laboratory experiments indicate that higher self-esteem can help people with persistence in a difficult task.[10]

SELF-ESTEEM, HUMILITY, AND SCRIPTURE

If self-esteem is a concept worth saving, then at this point, we should wonder what Scripture has to contribute to this conversation. We want the Bible to shape how we think about ourselves and how we encourage others under our care to think about themselves. Discerning the Bible's message here is a bit of a challenge, because self-esteem is hardly a trait that gets widespread treatment across the biblical witness, especially if we are looking for the individualistic expression of the concept. Remember, the concept in the way we understand it is only about 140 years old. But even if there are no explicit treatments of this modern concept, it actually speaks quite exquisitely to the same underlying ideas supporting the concept of self-esteem.

Israel's Self-Esteem and Ours

In the previous chapter, we saw that Ps 8 depicts humanity generally as having special worth and significance—our species has been "crowned with glory and honor" and has been given dominion over the rest of God's good creation. This surely speaks at least to some degree to a kind of self-esteem that all humans should have as God's special creatures.

This is a fine start. But it is in the story of Israel that we see the real struggle with something like self-esteem emerge. Many times throughout the Pentateuch, for example, Moses emphasizes that Israel was not selected by YHWH because of any special worthiness. He states bluntly they had no special strength, righteousness, or greatness that caused them to catch the divine eye (Deut 7:6–8; 9:4–6). On the contrary, Moses reiterates that their selection as the means of God's blessing to the wider world is due simply to God's

10. Baumeister et al., "Does High Self-Esteem," 14–15.

good pleasure and even hints that their smallness and stubbornness might have played a role.

Deuteronomy also records multiple warnings from Moses against Israel developing an overly positive self-evaluation after they arrive in the promised land. He predicts that when they experience commercial success in the land, they will be tempted to look at their prosperity and take credit for it, believing they are the reason for their flourishing. "Take care," Moses tells Israel,

> lest you forget the Lord your God by not keeping his commandments and his rules and his statutes, which I command you today, lest, when you have eaten and are full and have built good houses and live in them, and when your herds and flocks multiply and your silver and gold is multiplied and all that you have is multiplied, then your heart *be lifted up*, and you forget the Lord your God . . . who fed you in the wilderness with manna that your fathers did not know, *that he might humble you* and test you, to do you good in the end. Beware lest you say in your heart, "My power and the might of my hand have gotten me this wealth." You shall remember the Lord your God, for it is he who gives you power to get wealth, that he may confirm his covenant that he swore to your fathers, as it is this day. (Deut 8:11–18)

Notice the visual imagery here. Moses is concerned that Israel's heart will be "lifted up," a phrase that in this case refers to the exaltation that comes along with pride. And his exhortation is to remember that Yhwh is the reason for their prosperity and success but also that part of the divine project in the wilderness was to "humble" them (literally, "to bring them low"), which he says was for their good in the end. Similar warnings are repeated throughout the Old Testament at various times, and taken together, they suggest that self-esteem has a dangerous potential side effect; we can sometimes gain a positive self-evaluation at the cost of forgetting divine goodness.

And yet, self-esteem also gets some boosts throughout Israel's story. Just a few chapters before the warnings, Deuteronomy records Moses giving the Israelites reasons to think highly of themselves. He prophesies that when the nations hear about Israel, they will first cower in fear (Deut 2:25) and then stand in awe and admiration, saying, "'Surely this great nation is a wise and understanding people.' For what great nation is there that has a god so near to it as the Lord our God is to us, whenever we call upon him? And what great nation is there, that has statutes and rules so righteous as all this law that I set before you today?" (4:6–8). Based on these texts, Moses seems to be telling Israel in advance: you should expect some great things in your future, and you will know that you are special among all the peoples of the earth.

As we turn through the pages of the Old Testament, we see this promise is fulfilled—in terms of both God's blessing of Israel and their awareness of it. For example, at a high point in Israel's history, King David asks, "Who is like your people Israel, the one nation on earth whom God went to redeem to be his people?" (2 Sam 7:23). And even in darker times, when the prophets speak plenty of judgment to Israel, they also highlight the future good for which Israel is destined. Isaiah prophesies that in days of darkness all over the earth, Israel will be a beacon: "Nations shall come to your light, and kings to the brightness of your rising. . . . Then you shall see and be radiant; your heart shall thrill and exult, because the abundance of the sea shall be turned to you, the wealth of the nations shall come to you" (Isa 60:3, 5). In the verses that follow, Israel is predicted to be a bastion not only of prosperity but also of justice. They will be the center of a global movement in which the hungry are fed, the poor are no longer victims of unjust labor, and the enslaved are liberated from their chains (61:1–4). Such conditions are surely worthy of a positive self-assessment, aren't they?

Let's synthesize what we have seen so far. From the very beginning of Israel's existence as a nation, they live with a tension: on the one hand, they are a special group of people, chosen by God to be the recipients of his revelation through the Law and the Prophets, and the hosts of his special presence in the temple. In short, they are the *focus* and *locus* of God's work of redeeming and restoring all things, and they ought to have a strong sense of their communal self-worth, and they are even called to celebrate this in their common life.

Yet on the other hand, they are warned from the very beginning of the great risk of their special status: pride. Moses and the prophets warn them that this risk is so great that it actually has the power to undo much of what made them special in the first place, especially because their success may lead them to forget God's goodness to them.

Before we look at how these ideas get developed in the New Testament, let's just note here that this same tension arises, at least in some sense, for every Christian. We have each been drawn into God's household, inheriting the infinite riches of God's grace and having become bearers of God's Spirit. Aside from these things—which, let's be honest, sound very spiritual—Scripture tells us that God is working concrete good in our lives. As we become more patient and self-controlled people; as we grow in grace and generosity toward our neighbors; as we break free from addictions and help others get free too; in all of these things, there is something very right about looking back and celebrating this success.

And yet, like Israel, we must somehow regard this sense of what we would even call "pride" today with some wariness, knowing that we are always only a few steps away from the risk of self-exaltation.

The New Testament's Case for Holy Boasting

In his Letter to the Romans, Paul grapples with the tension between national pride and humility, and also with the question of how Gentiles should feel as the recipients of God's favor and grace extended in Christ. Here, we get some important additional context for understanding how to think about self-esteem and humility.

Near the beginning of his letter, Paul notes that some of his Jewish readers—that is, those who had been raised as Jews but had come to follow Christ as Messiah—have a kind of personal and national pride: they "rely on the law and boast in God" (Rom

2:17). The idea Paul seems to be getting at is this: some Jews were arguing that they had special reasons to be proud of their identity as God's chosen people. After all, they were the ones whom Yhwh had chosen as his instrument for bringing the nations to himself, as Paul himself notes in Rom 3:1–2, echoing Deut 4:6–8.

In spite of this, Paul will go on to argue that Jews are ultimately on the same footing as Gentiles when it comes to boasting before God. The Jews may "rely on the law and boast in God" (Rom 2:17), but they also "dishonor God by breaking the law" (2:23). Thus, "all, both Jews and Greeks, are under sin," falling far short of the divine demand of holiness (3:9). Because of this, Paul argues, "boasting" is excluded for all of us (3:27).

But this is not the end of the matter. Just two chapters later, Paul uses the same verb but this time in a positive sense: when he wants to describe the glory and richness of the peace with and access to God provided by Jesus, he says that we "boast" (most English translations use the word "rejoice" here because "boast" has uniformly negative connotations in English) "in the hope of the glory of God" (Rom 5:2). In addition, we "boast" in suffering, knowing that this also produces ultimately good results (5:3). He repeats it yet again a few verses later, noting that we can "boast" in the reconciliation we gain in Christ (5:11).

What is going on here? On the one hand, Paul is saying that we have no room for boasting; on the other hand, he is saying that we can and should boast! This paradox is not unique to Romans. In a letter to the Corinthians, Paul argues that God has chosen the things considered foolish and shameful to reveal his glory, "so that no human being may boast in the presence of God" (1 Cor 1:29), only to say two verses later that those who boast should "boast in the Lord" (1:31). This phrase gets repeated in the argument in 2 Cor 10–11, where Paul debates the value of his ministry in comparison with so-called "super-apostles," and argues that it is our weaknesses and suffering that are ultimately worthy of "boasting" (2 Cor 11:30; 12:5, 9).

What are we to make of all this back-and-forth? Do we boast or not boast? Or, put more modernly, should our self-esteem grow when we see what God is doing in us or not? The key to understanding Paul's arguments may be a passage from Jeremiah that Paul likely had in mind when he wrote all of these things.

In a section in which the prophet offers a scathing condemnation of Judah for their unfaithfulness to their covenant with God, he writes the following: "Let not the wise man boast in his wisdom, let not the mighty man boast in his might, let not the rich man boast in his riches, but let him who boasts boast in this, that he understands and knows me, that I am the Lord who practices steadfast love, justice, and righteousness in the earth. For in these things I delight, declares the Lord" (Jer 9:23–24).

Did you catch that?

The problem with most boasting, according to Jeremiah and Paul, is not so much the boasting in itself. Instead, the issue is where we find the basis for our boasting. As Jeremiah illustrates, in the context of divine judgment, whatever excellences may be the basis for our self-esteem and boasting are revealed to be simply insufficient.

So here is the key to the puzzle: only acquaintance and friendship with God are ultimately of enduring worth, and so these provide the only safe basis for our self-worth. Thus, every time Paul argues in favor of "boasting," he is doing it on the basis of his knowledge of and fellowship with the triune God. To put it in more modern terms: Paul is telling us that he has finally found a basis for self-esteem that is not shifting sand. This was the secret of "holy self-esteem" for Israel, and as Paul demonstrates, it remains a key insight for Christians today.

HUMILITY AND THE REDEMPTION OF SELF-ESTEEM

Notice how this biblical picture of self-esteem contrasts in important ways with the definitions we considered earlier. Recall that William James defined self-esteem as "success divided by pretensions," and Nathaniel Branden saw self-esteem as a stubborn insistence that one *simply is* both competent and worthy. Despite their differences with each other, both James and Branden ultimately hoped to solve our self-esteem problems by pointing us *inward*, urging us simply to view ourselves as more capable (Branden) or to abandon some of our aspirations (James).

In contrast, without forbidding honest self-assessment, the biblical vision for self-esteem primarily presses us to look *upward*: to assess ourselves first and foremost with reference to our proximity to our creator. This means that all the things on which our self-esteem generally hangs—our physical strength, our wisdom, our connections, our achievements, and so on—are simply the wrong units of measurement. Using these as our ultimate measuring rods is no more helpful than measuring weight in inches or time in gallons.

This does not mean blindness to our accomplishments or excellences. God does not ask us to be self-deceived or to somehow trick ourselves into overlooking our accomplishments. When we find that we are displaying the excellences to which human beings are called, we are no closer to healthy self-esteem—or, as we will see, to humility—if we attempt to "unknow" these things. Instead, the biblical vision for these things demands that all of these traits be relativized, put into perspective by our interactions with the triune God.

In fact, when we actually believe that the most important thing about us is, as Jeremiah puts it, the degree to which we "understand and know" our Creator, then we have the freedom to assess ourselves in all kinds of other areas—our performance at work, our physical fitness, our fulfillment of family duties—with frank honesty and authentic humility, unhindered by fear of what we may find. This ironclad security of self is what William James saw in Christians who had a kind of freedom from pretension that he admired, and it is the kind of self-assurance that can unleash our potential, which Branden sought; and it goes far deeper than the superficial self-esteem interventions that Baumeister demonstrated to be relatively meaningless.

CONCLUSION: HUMILITY AND SELF-ESTEEM IN REAL LIFE

What would it look like to navigate the ups and downs of life with authentic humility and a sense of self-esteem rooted fundamentally in our relationship with the triune God? We can see the upshot of this vision in three areas: how we receive praise, how we give praise, and how we respond to major failures.

To begin, it should mean that we are able to respond to the praise of others with gracious, balanced acceptance. Two factors that we've uncovered in this chapter are of help here. First, remember the biblical story teaches us that *all of our accomplishments and excellencies are ultimately gifts from God's hand*, the result of his Spirit working within us the good works he has "prepared in advance for us to do" (Eph 2:10 NIV). Like Israel, we acknowledge that God has chosen to make us examples of his goodness out of sheer grace and not because we were especially good material for God's planned work. So whatever is praiseworthy in us is the product of God's grace, often worked through others, which means we ought to respond to compliments in part by acknowledging our debt to others and to God.

But aside from acknowledging our debts to others and to God, responding to compliments with humility also means recognizing that our accomplishments and gifts must never be our ultimate measuring rod. Instead, we find the basis for our sense of self fundamentally in our relationship with the triune God, and in comparison to this, we consider all of our other accomplishments to be relatively minor details about us.

Of course, none of this should lead Christians to become excessively pious compliment receivers. We need not explain to everyone, every time, all the theological ins and outs of how we are processing their praise. Often, given social norms, a simple and genuine thank-you is just fine; but the greater the compliment and the more important it is to us, the more critical it is to filter our reaction through the lens of humility and redeemed self-esteem.

We have reflected so far on how to *receive* praise. But we should also reflect on how a Christian vision of humility and self-esteem should transform our vision for *giving* praise to those in our community and under our care. As a community concerned with cultivating humility, should we be hesitant to compliment one another or to strengthen the self-esteem of our children with regular doses of praise and encouragement? As strange as it may sound, this is a natural question that arises when we keep in mind that the power of pride and flattery is a serious risk to spiritual health.

But one of the beautiful things about the biblical vision of humility and self-esteem that we have uncovered in this chapter is that it neutralizes the most dangerous part of the self-esteem virus, making it safe to praise one another with total sincerity and unhindered generosity. Think about it this way: When praise means the world to us—that is, when our world rises or falls based entirely on how much praise or criticism we receive—we live entirely at the mercy of our performance and others' recognition of it. Equally importantly, we find ourselves competing with others for the limelight because we can feel safe and strong only when we are being honored.

In families and communities built on this approach to life, we are set up to suffer from the vices of pride and vainglory when we do well and to be utterly shattered when we miss expectations. In this type of community, everyone is in a zero-sum competition with everyone else; compliments are deployed only when strategically advantageous, ensuring that no one gains too much power and that the compliment giver receives something in return.

Now imagine a family, workplace, or church in which each person sees their ultimate worth as rooted in their relationship with the triune God. The biggest difference in this community is that praise just does not hold as much power over everyone. Each person is not bracing for their next compliment-driven high; instead, they can press along steadily because they know that their worth and identity are already secure. People in such a community have learned to pray, as the Book of Common Prayer puts it, "to fear nothing but the loss of you."[11] Families and churches grounded in this sense of identity can become the safest and most welcoming places on earth. In such communities, we are liberated from the need to impress one another, and we are freed to praise each other without fear of somehow diminishing our own status. In such communities, admiring one another sincerely can be the norm, precisely because the power of compliments has been relativized.

The power of failure is relativized too. In fact, communities that cultivate true humility and redeemed self-esteem ensure that even the grandest failure does not ultimately lead to unhealthy shame and humiliation. Firmly anchored in friendship with God, we can face even our most stinging defeats with confident poise, knowing that our identity is secure and our worth is undiminished. In communities like this, we can fully embrace Jesus's teaching that it is to the "poor in Spirit" that the kingdom of heaven belongs (Matt 5:3), and we can say along with Paul in total sincerity that "I delight in weaknesses, in insults, in hardships, in persecutions, in difficulties. For when I am weak, then I am strong" (2 Cor 12:10 NIV).

11. Episcopal Church, *Book of Common Prayer*, 216.

CHAPTER 4

Humble Confidence

Understanding Humility and Religious Conviction

"Religion and politics are topics that should never be introduced into general conversation," wrote John Young in 1882, "for they are subjects dangerous to harmony. Persons are most likely to differ, and least likely to preserve their tempers on these topics."[1] This has apparently been standard etiquette in the United States for at least 150 years, but when I moved to the United States after growing up in southeast Asia—where the rules of etiquette in this regard are generally more lenient—I remember how perplexed it left me. From my perspective, it seemed that this rule was almost designed to keep conversations as meaningless and shallow as possible.

Years later, after violating the rule more times than I care to admit—what's a theologian to do?—I acquired more sympathy for whoever thought it up. These subjects can be explosive in ways we might not expect, and it's often nearly impossible to have a productive resolution of even the smallest religious or political disagreements. Whether you're disagreeing with Christians or non-Christians, arguing about matters of faith is extremely difficult.

1. Young, *Our Deportment*, 91–92.

Yet it's not a task we can easily duck. One reality of modern life is that we are increasingly likely to interact with people who disagree with us about our faith. As nondenominational church movements have expanded in recent decades, it's increasingly likely that the person in the pew in front of you may disagree with your beliefs about intra-Christian debates, such as the proper mode of baptism, the best Bible translation, or how Christianity should inform political involvement. Even more significantly, changing migration and travel patterns have brought most people into much greater contact with sincere adherents of other faiths.

In these situations, most people sense a conflict between the Christian commitment to humility on the one hand, and our desire to hold our beliefs with firmness and courage on the other. In this chapter, we'll examine how the Bible leads us to think about humility and our faith commitments and see whether we can bring some resolution to the very real challenges that we often face in this area.

THE ARROGANCE OF FAITH

I remember vividly the first time I confronted the problem of how humility applies to matters of faith. I grew up in a town in the southern Philippines that was home to a significant Muslim minority population. My siblings and I ran with a group of kids in the neighborhood from Muslim households, and as we grew up together, we increasingly became aware of how different our faiths were and how the truth claims of each one explicitly conflicted with the other. Though we never squabbled over our religious differences, it struck me as a child that we and our Muslim friends stood in an awkward position—while we loved and respected each other a great deal, at the end of the day we each had to look at the other and think, "As far as I can tell, you are wrong about the fundamental direction and orientation of your life." Surely only the insanely arrogant would have the audacity to affirm such a claim, right?

The most popular approach to resolving such challenges at the moment is to minimize the differences between the Christian faith and other belief systems. We can choose to focus on the things that unite most religious groups, such as the appeal to love others, to protect the marginalized, and to find something holy in a world gone astray. In this frame, the problem of Christian arrogance is eliminated by the assertion that all religious traditions are equally enlightening, inspiring, and fruitful. They are little more than different paths up the same mountain, distinctive in their own ways but identical in their aim and equal in their effects.

At first glance, this seems to bring us to a place of humility. We follow the path laid out for us by Jesus but accept that we may be wrong and our neighbors of other faiths may be right. But while this approach seems to resolve the problem of religious arrogance, it creates another problem: it diminishes the truth claims and convictions that most religious people hold dear, reducing them to something like an aesthetic preference—just as some prefer Bach and others the Beatles, so some prefer the Buddha and others Muhammad. Of course, this is a way of looking at religion that is fundamentally at odds with most serious believers in any faith. Neither my Muslim friends nor I could affirm that our faiths were simply flavor preferences. Serious believers of various faiths have genuine and important disagreements about the nature of reality that shape the way they pray, worship, and conduct their daily lives.

In addition to failing to take our neighbors' faith seriously, this approach to religious humility makes it hard to see how Jesus could be the ultimate model of humility. If Jesus embodies humility, surely he should have been a first-century advocate of religious pluralism and tolerance—a view that was actually quite popular in the ancient world. Instead, Jesus often condemns his opponents as being dead wrong in their beliefs about God, even if he also demonstrates surprising love and compassion in the process. This applies whether he is dealing with people in his own faith, such as his rebuke of the Pharisees in Matt 23, or appealing to those of other faith backgrounds to follow him, such as when he interacts with the Samaritan woman in John 4:1–26.

So if humility with regard to our faith is not simply a matter of admitting that our views are preferences rather than claims to truth, what *does* it require of us? How can we engage those who have different views of God—whether they are from another faith altogether or simply from another branch of Christianity—with both humility and conviction? Building off what we've learned about humility so far, I want to propose that there are two essential ways that faith can be marked by authentic humility. First, we must recognize our ability to learn from others, even when they disagree with us. Because we are creatures with limits and the blindness of heart that comes from our entanglement with sin, we should be open to learning important things from our neighbors, even if we disagree with them on matters as great as how many true gods there are. Second, we must learn to bear joyful witness to what God has revealed to us while acknowledging unflinchingly what we do not know.

LEARNING TO RELY ON OTHERS

Moving to a foreign country may be one of the quickest ways to build your humility muscles. In talking with a friend who moved his family to Tokyo from their home in suburban Chicago, I couldn't help but notice how his sudden inability to care for himself resembled a return to infancy. When he was trying to order food at a restaurant or to describe his symptoms to a doctor, crucial matters were suddenly impossible to communicate. While he had always been a competent navigator back home, the complex rules of Japanese driving and his incomprehension of roadway signs would often leave him hopelessly disoriented. Cultural customs that even young children understood left him perplexed, and more than once he unintentionally offended others by violating social norms. In almost every aspect of his life he became utterly dependent on others who could help him navigate life in a new place.

This sense of our total helplessness is precisely what Jesus referred to when he told his disciples that "unless you turn and become like children, you will never enter the kingdom of heaven" (Matt 18:3). Rather than suggesting that his followers needed to have blind, uninformed, or ignorant faith—a common misunderstanding of this passage—Jesus seems to be teaching that his followers must gain a grasp of their relative helplessness in relation to their creator. They need to recognize that God is their Father, on whom they are dependent for their every need. This is, at least in part, what it means to cultivate humility.

But as we have seen, the Bible does not conceive of humility as a solely "vertical" reality. It has "horizontal" implications, too, as we are called not only to humble ourselves before God but also to exercise humility in relation to others. My friend in Tokyo learned this in radical ways in his first few months there. Over and over, Japanese people came to his rescue, explaining how to navigate a train schedule, helping him figure out how to get the right food, or helping him communicate about his health with a doctor. Of course, because Christians in Japan represent a slim minority of the population, this often meant depending on people who were not Christians. In fact, he was experiencing exactly the reverse of what many people think of as the nature of missions—rather than offering aid to non-Christians who were in need, he was the vulnerable one, receiving aid from his non-believing neighbors.

Finding Truth Among the Egyptians

Jesus and his family were no strangers to this phenomenon. The Gospel according to Matthew tells us that they spent several years in Egypt in the early part of Jesus's life hiding from Herod the Great (Matt 2:13–23). Given the brevity of Matthew's account, it's impossible to speculate about exactly what their life looked like during this time. But like any refugees fleeing persecution, we can be sure that Jesus and his family depended significantly on the hospitality of those who did not share their language, ethnicity, or faith.

While Matthew doesn't record any of the details of how they depended on their neighbors in this time, he does recount Mary and Joseph's response to at least one offer of significant aid from a group of non-Jews: namely, the magi. As faithful Jews, they could easily have refused the visit of the magi out of a concern to maintain adequate distance from followers of a pagan faith. Yet instead they received their gifts with gratitude and probably relied on their economic value for several years (Matt 2:1–12).

Christians have long looked at these events as metaphors rooted in the Old Testament that have enduring implications for the way we relate to those who are outsiders to the covenant. Just as the Jews built the tabernacle with the spoils of their former masters in Egypt, Christians have argued that we should be willing to accept what our neighbors have to offer us, whether it is material goods, assistance getting to the doctor, or deeper understanding of the world around us. We see this idea as early as second-century apologist Justin Martyr, who made a point of noting that whatever true knowledge our non-Christian counterparts have is suitable for Christian use too.[2]

Augustine also wrote about this idea extensively in a work designed to help Christians understand what it meant to follow Christ in a pagan context. He writes:

> If those, however, who are called philosophers happen to have said anything that is true, and agreeable to our faith, the Platonists above all, not only should we not be afraid of them, but we should even *claim back for our own use* what they have said, as from its unjust possessors. It is like the Egyptians, who not only had idols and heavy burdens, which the people of Israel abominated and fled from, but also vessels and ornaments of gold and silver, and fine raiment, which the people secretly appropriated for their own. . . . In the same way, while the heathen certainly have counterfeit and superstitious fictions in all their teachings . . . their teachings also contain liberal disciplines which are more suited to the service of the truth, as well as a number of most useful ethical principles, and *some true things are to be found among them about worshiping only the one God.*[3]

While it may not be obvious, Augustine is laying the groundwork here for humble interaction with those who disagree with our faith. It starts with admitting that we do not have a monopoly

2. Justin Martyr, *2 Apol.* 13.3.

3. Augustine, *Teaching Christianity*, 159–60; emphasis added.

on truth. All truth belongs to its creator—and just as anyone can find a concentration of precious metal in the earth, by God's grace and providence, people from any faith background have access to truth. Moreover, while Augustine starts by focusing on how we can learn about math, science, and history from our non-Christian counterparts, in this section he goes so far as to suggest that Christians stand to gain from non-Christians in the areas of ethics and theology. This is a breathtaking statement, especially coming from Augustine, who thoroughly repudiated the misguided ethics and theology of his old life when he became a believer.

I think something like Augustine's attitude toward other faith traditions is a necessary prerequisite for humble interaction with our Muslim, Buddhist, or Hindu (or atheist or agnostic) neighbors. Rather than entering such conversations with self-assurance that we are the only ones with something to offer, we should remain open to the possibility that we have important things to gain by understanding their worldview, their approach to ethics, or even their understanding of God. We should be open to the possibility that by God's providence and grace, they have found a vein of truth that we had previously overlooked. We should resist the temptation to view ourselves only as generous benefactors in such conversations and be willing also to be recipients of what our neighbors have to offer.

Ultimately, a willingness to learn from our non-believing neighbors is grounded in a deep theological truth: that all people are created in the image of God, and while the image may be marred or obscured by sin, it is never eliminated. Acknowledging this reality can transform the way these interactions go. Theologian John Stackhouse points out that it allows us to "adopt the voice of a friend who thinks he has found something worth sharing but recognizes that not everyone will agree on its value. . . . We should sound like we really do respect the intelligence, and spiritual interest, and moral integrity of our neighbors."[4] When we approach our neighbors with authentic, unfeigned humility, we don't just increase the persuasiveness of our message; we also allow the

4. Stackhouse, *Humble Apologetics*, 229.

medium to match the message. It is a wicked irony that Christian apologetics so often takes on a proud, self-satisfying tone, when it is ultimately an invitation to follow the way of Jesus, the consummate servant and paragon of humility.

Before we move on to point to an additional way that humility should shape our faith disagreements, we need to dispel two possible misunderstandings of what has been said so far. First, it may be tempting at this point in the chapter to think that humility about our faith must mean that we need to look beyond Christ himself to understand who God is, how to have peace with God, or any number of spiritual matters. But this is exactly the kind of false teaching that Paul debunks in his letter to the Colossians, where he urges Christians not to be "taken captive" by human traditions, precisely because it is in Christ alone that "all the fullness of God was pleased to dwell" (Col 1:19; 2:9). Paul here echoes the Old Testament prophets, who warned Israel against thinking that they needed supplementary deities. As Isaiah notes, false gods are really no gods at all—they have eyes that do not see and ears that do not hear, and those who worship them become like them (see Isa 44–45). Given the Bible's clarity here, we cannot rightly suggest that there are, hidden in these other traditions, pieces of the spiritual puzzle that we have not already been given.

But this does not mean that our non-believing neighbors have nothing to offer us of worth. To continue the analogy of a jigsaw puzzle, while we can say with certainty that we need not go searching among other faith traditions in order to find pieces that were not given to us in Christ, we may learn from our neighbors to recognize pieces of the puzzle that we were ignoring before or discern ways they fit together to which we had previously been blind.

For example, I came to understand the notion of atoning sacrifice in new ways only after talking with a friend who came from a non-Christian background where his family actually made regular sacrificial offerings. Similarly, we may find that our non-Christian neighbors have a way of assembling the pieces of the puzzle in ways we didn't expect. Thomas Aquinas, for example, found in Aristotle's thinking a helpful way of organizing human knowledge of everything from biology to ethics, even though Aristotle knew nothing of Jesus and would probably have rejected him if he had met him.

The second possible misunderstanding we must rule out is the notion that humility about religious belief must lead us to something like a "blind men and elephant" situation. This is the analogy that many advocates of religious pluralism employ to suggest that all of the various faiths are simply grabbing onto a different part of the true God and magnifying that aspect as the only truth, just as several blind men might each grasp a different part of an elephant—its trunk, its leg, its torso—and conclude that they are touching, respectively, a snake, a tree trunk, or a boulder. Though the analogy may be simplistic, it has considerable explanatory power for many people. With some humility—a willingness to admit the limitations of our own tradition—we can recognize the noble and true aspects of every faith, protecting our ability to treat all faiths with equality and respect.

But as we noted above, it's impossible for this view to embody true respect for devout neighbors, since it implies that their closely held beliefs are little more than flavor preferences. Nor does it embody specifically *Christian* humility, since it fails to take Jesus's model of humility seriously and undermines the particular truth claims that Jesus makes. He depicts himself as not merely one path among others but as *the* way, truth, and life (John 14:6). His atoning death does not merely offer a potential for a solution of sin and its problems; it is the *only* permanent resolution in history (Heb 10).

WRESTLING WITH OUR LIMITATIONS

So if a humble faith cannot be merely about reducing our confidence levels, how *should* humility shape the way we think about our beliefs? So far, we've mainly focused on how humility should mark our tone and personal approach to religious disagreement. But in addition to being willing to learn from our neighbors, Christian humility requires something else: an awareness of the limits of our theological understanding, or intellectual humility with respect to our theological convictions.

In recent years, psychologists, philosophers, and theologians have focused intense attention on intellectual humility. There is continuing debate about how best to define this concept, but an influential definition is that *intellectual humility* "consists in proper attentiveness to, and owning of, one's intellectual limitations."[5] According to researchers, this trait is one of the most potent predictors of all kinds of good things: it is associated with intellectual curiosity, openness to new ideas, tolerance of ambiguity, better assessment of arguments, and a willingness to change one's mind when faced with new facts.[6] It helps us react in more constructive ways to religious disagreements,[7] and to be more ready to forgive others in the wake of religious conflict.[8] Pastors and other religious leaders who demonstrate intellectual humility are more trusted than those who appear to lack it.[9]

This growing body of research demonstrating intellectual humility's benefits should be viewed as a victory for a Christian idea. It is the *mind* of Christ that Paul highlights when he calls for the Philippians to follow their savior's humble example (Phil 2:5), just after he asks believers to be of the same *mind* (2:2) and to *think* of others ahead of themselves (2:3). In some of the earliest Christian writings, we see emphasis not only on humility generally but also on humility of *mind*, which can protect Christians from the dangers of hubris.[10]

A few centuries later, in the hands of Augustine, this idea receives further development. Ever a student of language, Augustine

5. Whitcomb et al., "Intellectual Humility," 520.

6. Leary et al., "Cognitive and Interpersonal Features."

7. Kross and Grossmann, "Boosting Wisdom"; Hopkin et al., "Intellectual Humility and Reactions."

8. Zhang et al., "Intellectual Humility and Forgiveness."

9. McElroy et al., "Intellectual Humility."

10. See, e.g., Clement of Rome, who writes: "You see, dear friends, the kind of pattern that has been given to us; for if the Lord so humbled himself, what should we do, who through him have come under the yoke of his grace?" (1 Clem. 16:17 [Holmes, *Apostolic Fathers*, 50]).

frequently struggles with the degree to which our words for God, however elegant and powerful, will always fall short of adequately describing our maker and redeemer: "I grieve over the inability which my tongue has betrayed in answering to my heart," he says, admitting that even with all his rhetorical training, his words are never fully up to the task of theological discussion.[11] Of course, he hardly lets this stop him from speaking and writing about God; we are called to worship and proclaim the triune God with all the sincerity, care, and profundity that our abilities allow. But we pursue these tasks always aware of our limitations; in other words, we worship, pray, and preach with intellectual humility.

Augustine's view of this is grounded in the Bible's view of humanity. Recall what we learned in chapter 2, when we considered the Bible's vision for humility. We saw there that the Christian Scriptures conceive of humans as finite, fallen creatures. Though we were created for glory, we are but a small part of an enormous universe and have brought ourselves low through our entanglement with sin. Though God speaks to us clearly and consistently through the prophets and the apostles, our finitude and our fallenness mean that our knowledge of God this side of eternity is limited rather than comprehensive (because of finitude) and can be mistaken (because of our fallenness).

But what distinguishes Augustine's view of intellectual humility from most contemporary accounts is his understanding of two matters: grace and time. While he acknowledges that our minds, hearts, and language are limited, he is equally confident that divine grace has an amazing way of empowering us to know God ever more deeply through his Word and his Spirit. Because God reveals himself and illumines our minds, we come to know God through never-ending cycles of deeper knowledge, followed by recognition of our limits, followed by deeper knowledge yet again. In a beautiful passage, he writes that knowledge of God is "sought in order to be found all the more delightfully," and "found in order to be sought all the more avidly."[12] We need never throw up our hands

11. Augustine, *On the Catechizing* 2.3 (*NPNF*[1] 3:284).

12. Augustine, *Trinity*, 396.

in resignation to ignorance, in other words, because even the most sublime mysteries can be opened to us slowly but surely through God's gracious revelation.

Just as important as this robust view of grace, however, is Augustine's sense of how time impacts our knowledge of God. Augustine is aware that Scripture depicts humanity's knowledge of God unfolding differently across three distinctive eras. In the first era—the time before Christ—mysteries abounded, and we knew God only in part. Those within the Abrahamic covenant had enough information to commune with the one true God, though only temporarily, through the temple and the sacrificial system.

When Christ came, "the mystery hidden for ages and generations" (Col 1:26)—God's plan for the nations, as well as his very identity—was revealed. Jesus's coming inaugurated a second phase of history, offering humans a qualitatively different kind of knowledge of God. This idea—that we are able to know God in a deeper, surer way because of Jesus—is all over the New Testament. In his conversation with the Samaritan woman, for example, Jesus highlights the fact that knowledge of God has not always been easy to come by, especially for outsiders. The woman expresses the expectation of the Jews when she says, "I know that Messiah is coming (he who is called Christ). When he comes, he will tell us all things" (John 4:25), at which point Jesus reveals that he is the one we've been waiting for.

The rest of the New Testament is replete with confirmation that we are indeed recipients of a better revelation than our Old Testament forebears. The author of Hebrews puts it this way: while God has always been communicating with his people through the prophets, in our time he has "spoken to us by his Son," who is "the radiance of the glory of God and the exact imprint of his nature" (Heb 1:1–3). Peter writes about how the Old Testament prophets "searched and inquired carefully," hoping to discover what we now know, good news into which "even angels long to look" (1 Pet 1:10–12 NIV). As these passages demonstrate, we have good reasons to be confident that because we know Jesus by the power of the Spirit, we know God in the truest possible sense.

But the New Testament also highlights the partialness of our current knowledge. We "know in part and we prophesy in part," Paul tells us, but eventually, "the partial will pass away." For now, we "see in a mirror dimly," but then we will see "face to face." He looks forward to the day when our knowledge of God will be similar in quality to God's knowledge of us (1 Cor 13:9–12). John similarly looks forward to the day when we will "see him [Jesus] as he is"; this kind of face-to-face knowledge, he says, will result in our transformation and final sanctification (1 John 3:2).

The point of these passages is to highlight that we are only in the second, rather than the final phase of human history. Though Christ has come, and through him God has spoken with clarity and finality, our redemption is not yet complete, and our acquaintance with God is not as full as it will one day be.

What does this all mean? It means that for Christians, humility about our faith does not require that we doubt our every belief or that we constantly question our convictions. But it does require that we read the eschatological clock correctly. Because we have not yet experienced final redemption and sanctification—because we, like the rest of creation, continue to yearn in anticipation of that day when we know Jesus face to face—we should be ready to confess the provisional nature of our knowledge in the meantime. We await that day with joyful, sunny confidence, but without the arrogant presumption that we have arrived.

HUMILITY IN ACTION: BEARING CONFIDENT AND HUMBLE WITNESS

Paul offers a fantastic example of what it looks like to be faithful as well as humble in talking with non-believing neighbors in Acts 17. There, he is interacting with a group of thoughtful Athenians whom the narrator Luke tells us are passionate about understanding the latest new ideas. Though they are skeptical of his message initially, they invite him to share, and he takes it up with a delightful mixture of confidence and humility.

He begins by complimenting his hosts. "People of Athens! I can see that in every way you are very religious" (Acts 17:22 NIV). He points to an idol in the corner that is inscribed "to an unknown god" and tells his audience that he is going to share with them the identity of this god that has previously been hidden. He goes on to describe the basics of the faith—that God is the maker of all things and that there is only one true creator God, etc.—but then surprises the crowd by quoting Epimenides and Aratus, two Greek philosophers who lived hundreds of years before Jesus and had no relationship to Judaism. Paul uses the quotation from Aratus ("We are his offspring") as the foundation for the rest of his argument: "Therefore since we are God's offspring," he argues, surely God must be something other than a gold or stone object (17:29).

Paul has nothing to fear in admitting that there is true knowledge of God to be found among his non-believing audience. He is happy to identify with them, at least in part, in their religious knowledge. "Being then God's offspring," he says in Acts 17:29, "*we* ought not to think that the divine being is like gold or silver or stone, an image formed by the art and imagination of man." But all the same, he can bear witness to the gospel of the crucified and risen Lord and do so with neither embarrassment—even though 17:32 suggests he likely knew there would be some snickering—nor false humility.

Lesslie Newbigin, a British missionary to India who became a teacher of theology and missions later in life, offers a similar model set in a time and culture closer to our own. Though he began his missionary career with a group that generally eschewed evangelism out of respect for other faith traditions, he soon became convinced that such timidity was not an option for Christians.

In doing so, he was fond of noting that early Christians always refused the temptation to make Christianity into a merely private cult. Movements that invited people to add a new faith commitment to their already existent convictions were common in the first century. Yet in contrast to these movements, early Christians recognized that they were making a fundamentally *public* rather than *private* claim when they confessed that Jesus is Lord.

Newbigin reflects that such a confession "implies a claim regarding the entire public life of mankind and the whole created world. . . . Like the claim of the scientist, with respect to his discoveries, it is a claim that the truth of what is believed will be confirmed in new discoveries that cannot be specified in advance."[13] In saying this, Newbigin is hoping to dispel the notion that we can approach our non-believing neighbors with the false humility that says "this is true for me but may not be for you" or fails to offer confident witness at all.

Importantly, Newbigin also pairs this advice with an equally strong commendation of humility that is stirring in the authenticity of its conviction. He notes, first of all, that times have changed dramatically from the early twentieth century, when many Western Christians had a misguided assurance that it was only a matter of time before "the whole world would receive its blessings."[14] Instead, the pattern of the moment is for non-believers to ask Christians what makes them think that they have some privileged information about the world that everyone else lacks. It is expected, and appropriate, for our neighbors to ask us the question that was often asked of Jesus: "By what authority" do you claim to tell me what I should believe?

Our response, Newbigin contends, must echo that of the apostles in Acts 4:7; when asked "by what power or what name" they were healing and sharing the gospel, they have no choice but to refer to "the name of Jesus." They *do* believe that they have information that their non-Christian counterparts do not have: namely, they have encountered in Jesus of Nazareth the ultimate revelation of the triune God.

Yet this is not because of some privilege conferred by ethnic or socioeconomic background, or long hours of formal study, or some special ability to discern what others have missed. Our confidence lies not in ourselves but in the one who says to his apostles, "You did not choose me, but I chose you and appointed you that you should go and bear fruit" (John 15:16).

13. Newbigin, *Open Secret*, 16.

14. Newbigin, *Open Secret*, 12.

Newbigin's next comment brings it all together and is worth quoting in full:

> I would be distorting the truth if I simply spoke of this confession as being mine alone. I make this confession only because I have been laid hold of by Another and commissioned to do so. It is not primarily or essentially my decision. By ways that are mysterious to me, that I can only faintly trace, I have been laid hold of by one greater than I and lead into a place where I must make this confession and where I find no way of making sense of my own life or of the life of the world except through being an obedient disciple of Jesus.[15]

This passage is one of the best that I have ever come across in terms of casting a vision for engaging in interreligious conversations with a spirit of authentic Christian humility. I love how it models a way of sharing our faith that does not shy away from the weight of Christianity's claims, acknowledging that the gospel will inevitably displace and compete with the key assertions of other religious traditions. At the same time, it sets these convictions in their proper context. They are not affirmations of our superiority to those of other faiths but are our only way of making sense of our experience of being caught up in the redeeming work of Christ and his Spirit.

Such a posture is by no means an evangelistic "silver bullet"; it will not (or at least not typically) persuade skeptics immediately to trust the Christian account of the universe over others. But it is a posture that, when paired with openness to learning from others, lays a sound foundation for genuine friendship with our neighbors from other faith traditions (or those from no religious tradition at all). Cultivating that kind of friendship is a central calling for Christians of every generation and place because it is precisely in such contexts that we are most effectively able to bear witness to the humbling, life-altering message of the gospel.

15. Newbigin, *Open Secret*, 17.

CHAPTER 5

Constraining Curiosity

How Humility Can Help Us Survive the New Information Age

IN THIRTEENTH-CENTURY PARIS, A renaissance in learning was underway. Near the city's renowned Notre Dame Cathedral, there was an emerging institution of higher learning that was not quite like anything that had gone before, with departments dedicated to various aspects of learning, a faculty with diverse areas of expertise, and an ever-increasing stable of books to document new research discoveries. Eventually, it would come to be known as one of the first universities in the world.

But a young, rising star member of the faculty—Thomas Aquinas, who would later come to be recognized as one of the greatest minds of his time—had a brewing concern. He noticed that while his students indeed had access to a wider stable of knowledge than ever before, they were not necessarily becoming wiser or better for it. Many were willing to prioritize obscure and irrelevant questions over matters that should have been much more central. They had lost sight of the purpose of their learning, often pursuing it for its own sake and without a moral compass. Most concerningly, he saw that students were starting to engage the intellectual world without reference to the God from whom all knowledge and wisdom spring. As a devoted follower of Jesus who sought to train students to consider all of life through the lens of their faith, he put his considerable intellect toward the task of helping his students navigate this new era of abundant knowledge with wisdom.

It's hard not to wonder how Thomas would feel about our world. We live in what is often called the *information age*, an era of history marked by an explosion of data and knowledge at a scale that would have been impossible to imagine in previous generations. New discoveries in every field of study are regularly celebrated as hallmarks of human progress. We have recently witnessed enormous breakthroughs in artificial intelligence, which advocates argue could be the most important development in history for helping humans push the boundaries of our learning ever further. If Thomas had good reason to be worried about how followers of Jesus could navigate the ever-expanding ocean of knowledge in his time, then we have far more.

Most of us can recognize in ourselves some echoes of Thomas's concern that more knowledge may not always make us better. We have felt it, for example, while reckoning with the groggy emptiness that comes from overdosing on online articles, social media, or videos. Even when these journeys begin with admirable quests for important information, diving down an online rabbit hole usually leaves us with more regret than useful knowledge or genuine wisdom. Or perhaps you have sensed that something is wrong with our state of information abundance when you see that the proliferation of disinformation and partisan spin mixed in with the good and true bits out there is causing us increasingly to throw up our hands and wonder whether we can really know much of anything.[1]

In a very real sense, we are experiencing in our lifetimes the very thing that Thomas foresaw and feared for his students in the thirteenth century. We have more knowledge available to us than ever before, but we lack a coherent framework to engage this knowledge in a way that can lead to our flourishing.

1. For helpful reflection on this phenomenon, see Kristian, *Untrustworthy*.

Yet even when we are alive to this problem in general terms, most of us struggle to explain it in a specific or coherent way. We may wonder: When we go down an internet rabbit hole or scroll social media too long, is our problem primarily that we are seeking too much knowledge or just the wrong kind? Or along similar lines: Is the solution to the misinformation and spin in media to simply read more news sources—or is this actually, as some studies suggest, likely to cause us to become even more susceptible to disinformation?

In short, we don't know how to tell whether our appetite for learning in any given case is healthy or harmful. So like a college student using their freedom from parental oversight to eat whatever their taste buds desire, we are in desperate need not only of limits but of a way of thinking about our intellectual diet that can help us survive the era of informational superabundance.

In this chapter we'll see that humility is in fact the keystone virtue that can help us navigate the complicated world of knowledge abundance that we face in the twenty-first century. This is because cultivating humility helps us foster a healthy relationship with our finitude and fallenness as God's creatures and to come to terms with our need for limits in a world of limitless information.

To begin, we'll start by considering Thomas's diagnosis of the problems we encounter when we pursue knowledge recklessly. Characteristic of Thomas, it is a careful and thorough analysis of the issue, identifying at least four ways that otherwise healthy love for learning can go wrong. As we consider these in turn, we'll see how humility is the key to keeping our bearings as we navigate a world awash in knowledge but short on wisdom.

THE WONDROUS RISE AND FALL OF CURIOSITY

Thomas was one of the most well-read and thoughtful people of his time, with interest not only in the biggest questions of philosophy, ethics, and theology but also in poetry, the arts, and the changes in scientific thinking of his time. In short, he was a nerd with an unusually formidable intellectual life. As a faculty member at the University of Paris, which was at the center of a transformation of advanced learning in Western Europe, Thomas clearly had an interest in advancing the state of human knowledge about the world and all it contains.

All of this should make it a bit surprising to read his critique of *curiositas*, a Latin term that closely resembles, though is not exactly the same as, the English word "curiosity." Joining his theological predecessors, Thomas thought of *curiositas* as an illness that distorts and misdirects our love of knowledge, and he believed his students could ignore it only at their own peril, especially in an environment where knowledge was ever more available.

Like a good spiritual doctor, he sought to help his students see exactly how their otherwise healthy longings to know could be distorted into unhealthy curiosity. In characteristically thorough and careful fashion, Thomas argued that there are four main ways that knowledge seeking can go wrong: (1) we can use it as a distraction, and it can thus pull us away from doing the things that God has called us to do; (2) we can seek to learn things dangerous to our well-being; (3) we can seek to know God's world without reference to God himself; and (4) we can seek to know things beyond our capacity. In a moment, we'll consider how each of these four tendencies manifests itself in our information age and how humility can help us navigate an increasingly rich and risky information environment.

But before we move on, we should pause to observe that since Thomas's time, curiosity has had an interesting ride in public opinion. Philosophers before and directly after Thomas considered it a serious threat to the good life, with some even considering *curiositas* to be a primary vice, as dangerous as pride or lust. But starting about four hundred years after Thomas's time, curiosity was increasingly treated as a virtue rather than a vice. In the twenty-first century, the notion of curiosity as a vice is almost farcical, and it is regarded by many as the *solution* to the modern situation of knowledge abundance, rather than a contributing *problem*.

Intriguingly, curiosity's ascent and descent in public opinion is the inverse of humility's reputation. In the fourth and fifth centuries, when curiosity's status as a vice was rising in Christendom, humility's status as a virtue was rising as well, with many thinkers in medieval Christianity arguing that humility was the primary virtue and many others suggesting *curiositas* was the primary vice. But during the Enlightenment, the two would trade places, as increasingly humility was viewed as a weakness—a residue of the old world or even a shackle that had kept humanity from achieving its full potential for centuries.[2]

We'll see in this chapter why this is no mere coincidence. After all, humility is the trait by which we train our hearts and minds to recognize and embrace our limitations, and so it makes sense that as Western culture increasingly placed a priority on throwing off the constraints on our knowledge, it also became increasingly dismissive of the idea that we should ever turn down the opportunity to gain new information.

It's important to remember that for Thomas, analyzing curiosity was no mere academic interest, nor was it an attempt to create a legalistic code of conduct for his students. Instead, it had everything to do with helping his students and readers apply their faith to a critical aspect of human life: growing in our knowledge of our creator and the world around us. As we'll see in this chapter, each of the dangers he highlighted is more than ever acute today, and humility is the most important tool we have for helping us to overcome them as we seek to know and follow Jesus of Nazareth. We'll start by looking at the first danger Thomas highlights for us: distraction.

CURIOSITY AS DISTRACTION

If Thomas thought thirteenth-century Paris posed a risk of information seeking going astray with its new wealth of available knowledge, we can only imagine how he would react to the circumstances of the twenty-first century. Far more new information

2. For a fascinating study of how curiosity was viewed as the Enlightenment dawned, see Kivistö, *Vices of Learning*.

is published today than ever before, and the media landscape includes more material than a human could consume in a lifetime. Of course, this is neither inherently good nor bad. But this historically unprecedented situation requires that we get a clear sense of what it means to engage in our quest for knowledge in a way that is consistent with our finitude and fallenness. In short, it requires that we think about how humility should shape the way we read, think, and come to know the world around us.

I am just old enough to remember when the worldwide web was first becoming popular, and I recall the brimming enthusiasm of the time about the incredible amount of information that it would place at our fingertips. Journalists and scholars glowed about the new "information superhighway," which would spirit us along into ever greater progress and deeper knowledge. Of course, in certain ways, these predictions have come true.

But it is also the case that the internet has become the distractor-in-chief for most of us. Especially when we need a diversion from stress, the allure of the information always at our fingertips can sometimes seem irresistible. At its worst, the availability and anonymity of the internet can draw us to places online where we know we should not be (more on that in the next section). Yet even when our time online is focused solely on benign or worthy pursuits—keeping up with friends via social media, learning about new ideas, or reading the news—we often fall prey to what Thomas describes. We too often neglect what God has called us to at any given time—being fully engaged at work, loving and serving our families, or having moments of quiet meditation—in order to pursue trivial knowledge about the news of the day or to watch videos of cats.

In a relatively short period, the internet and the proliferation of pocket-sized computers have transformed our habits of mind for the worse. Journalist Nicholas Carr documents this transformation beautifully in *The Shallows*, where he marshals evidence from psychology, neuroscience, and philosophy to help readers understand a phenomenon most of us have experienced: that our use of the internet has shortened our attention spans and weakened our ability to wrestle with deep and hard questions. Meanwhile, psychologist

Sherry Turkle has offered a nuanced but disturbing picture of how technology has come to shape our social lives, noting especially how we frequently allow the distraction of more surface-level interactions via social media to displace deeper face-to-face connections.[3]

For followers of Jesus who want to be all that they are called to be, these dangers—to our work life, social life, and habits of thinking—should cause concern. But perhaps the most serious danger posed by distraction is that it can keep us from the kind of quiet solitude that is often required to cultivate deep acquaintance with God. I suspect I'm not alone in finding that my phone-based Bible reading time too often gets hijacked by incoming notifications demanding my immediate attention.

Humility and the Discipline of Facing Our Limits

So how does a Christian vision of humility help us address the challenge of distraction? To begin, we should recall that Scripture's vision of humility entails understanding our finitude. In particular, Scripture often highlights the brevity of our lifespan, for example, by reminding us that our life is like a vapor (Eccl 1:2–4) and like grass consumed by a fire (Ps 103:15; 1 Pet 1:24). For this reason, the psalmist prays: "Show me, Lord, my life's end and the number of my days; let me know how fleeting my life is" (Ps 39:4–5 NIV). Similarly, Paul urges Christians to "redeem the time" because the Lord's arrival is near (Eph 5:16).

Put simply, Scripture reminds us that we are creatures, not gods, and we must organize our lives accordingly. In practical terms, this means that we cannot justify seeking to know anything and everything but must focus our knowledge seeking on those things that deserve the highest priority.[4]

This will require thinking carefully about what God has called us to do in any given season and then developing patterns of life that will remind us of our finitude. Sabbath rest is a practice

3. Turkle, *Alone Together*.

4. For excellent, practical guidance on this score, see McCracken, *Wisdom Pyramid*.

designed for precisely this purpose—as we take one day per week to create distance from our work (and maybe our screens), we allow ourselves to acknowledge and enjoy our status as creatures dependent on God's good care. In addition, most of us would benefit from creating barriers to distractions that are particularly tempting for us, whether by removing apps from our phones or creating "no-screen" times during which we force our distracted minds and hearts to focus. It may be wise for many of us to read Scripture from a physical Bible rather than from our devices, which can often introduce extraneous distractions into one of the most time deserving of our tasks.

Whatever practices we choose to implement, we should keep in mind that our goal is not simply to return to a simpler time, as if we could revert to some golden past before the internet and widespread computing "ruined us." Thomas's experience should remind us that distraction has always been a problem for humans, even if each generation introduces new iterations of the problem. Instead, we should focus on the reality that like Adam and Eve, we are tempted by the allure of false infinitude—being "like God"—and that our flourishing depends on a willing acknowledgment that we are not. In short, we can flourish in a world of unending distraction only by cultivating humility.

LEARNING FROM ILLICIT SOURCES

Aside from distraction, Thomas highlights another way that our longing to know can go awry: seeking to know things that are not consistent with our good.[5]

In the haunting 2014 film *Nightcrawler*, we meet Lou Bloom, a lonely con artist who finds his way into a job as a freelance

5. Close readers of Thomas may note that Thomas's initial focus in this section is technically on "those who seek to know the future through the demons" (Aquinas, *Summa Theologica*, II–II, q. 167, art. 1). However, in the next article in this section, Thomas also attends carefully to the ways that we may desire the wrong types of knowledge, and I am treating these two discussions together.

videographer for a Los Angeles news channel.[6] Early in the film, he recognizes that his job is primarily to give viewers what they long for: firsthand images of the tragedies that emerge in their communities in the darkness of night. By becoming the first person at the scene of a car accident, a homicide, or any number of gruesome events, he discovers that viewers are perversely drawn to especially violent images and stories. As he increasingly channels the audience's thirst for gore, he transforms from a small-time television stringer to a formidable force in the local media scene who knows what viewers want and who has an uncanny knack for finding it.

His quest to find the most tragic images to convey to his viewers is cloaked in virtue. Inquiring minds in the community want to know what a crime looks like as it happens or how a gruesome car crash is experienced by first responders. At least initially, Bloom is motivated by benign impulses: a desire for gainful employment and a thirst for the sense of dignity that owning one's own business can confer. Perhaps most poignantly, he communicates to others, and to himself, throughout the film that what he wants more than anything is to know the taste of true success—to gain acquaintance with a satisfaction that has always eluded him in his previous life.

Yet the film is full of warning signs that both Bloom's and his audience's quest for knowledge is tragically flawed. All the sane characters in the film recognize that there is something the matter with the quest to see ever-more-gruesome video, though they can never quite explain why. Bloom himself seems to lack enough self-awareness ever to doubt his own desires for knowing the taste of success, but the producer that he partners with is wracked with doubt and guilt over her role in sating the questionable desires of her viewing audience, even as she continues to go along with Bloom's schemes to push the envelope further each week. At the same time, the film's viewers are prompted to question their own desires to know, see, and experience the depravity of the main character as he hurtles toward his own gruesome end.

The film functions as a kind of parable about how our longing to know can be malformed and misdirected. In modern life, we

6. Gilroy, *Nightcrawler.*

teach our children to be as curious as possible, and we universally prefer those who are open-minded over those who do not expose themselves to the broad array of media available to us. To know something is always better than to not know it.

And so when new technology made it easy to record and share videos of violent events—police shootings, terrorist attacks, and the like—many of us felt there was something awry with viewing them, but because of our training to indiscriminately approve all longings to know, we have often simply conceded.

Of course, the old instincts are not entirely gone. Most people still disapprove of perverse pornographic images, for example, though without access to a religious moral framework, they often have trouble explaining why. When ISIS began tweeting gruesome footage of executions in 2015, many argued that they should not be shared and publicized, though again the reasons for this were tricky—was it because it was unethical, or simply because it would give a propaganda victory to terrorists? As we saw earlier, most of us simply lack a coherent framework to analyze and decide what kinds of knowledge are worth pursuing and what kinds should be off-limits to us.

Often, the Christian answer to this issue focuses on Paul's exhortation that we should fix our eyes on "whatever is true, whatever is honorable, whatever is just, whatever is pure, whatever is lovely, whatever is commendable" (Phil 4:8). As a reminder about what kinds of things should be the focus of our deep meditation, this is surely sound advice.

But it's too simplistic to rely on this statement as the only test for determining which books we should read, which art we should view, or which TV shows to watch. If we did, almost all study of history would be off-limits, since it often consists of reflecting on the impure, unlovely things that have happened before us (wars, betrayals, moral failings, etc.). Most fictional narratives, likewise, rely on telling us about the uncommendable; in fact, this is part of the unique way in which stories can expose deep truths about what it means to be good, true, or godly. Clearly then, there is some complexity here that we must attend to if we want to understand the ways in which our hearts can go astray in longing to know things they ought not know.

Humility and Our Broken Intellectual Appetites

It's here that our full-orbed account of humility has something to teach us. Earlier, we saw how humility can help us combat distraction by reminding us of our limited time and mental resources—by embracing our finitude. But in this case, humility helps in a different way—it prompts us to reckon with our entanglement with sin and vice, and to see how these have misdirected and misshapen our God-given longing to know. As we cultivate humility, we should be able to admit that many of our quests for knowledge are simply wrong, even when they are cloaked in a veneer of nobility. In short, humility requires that we look with clear eyes at the distorted topography of our hearts. and be ready to admit our intellectual motivations are complex and often more mistaken and sinful than we care at first to admit.

In practical terms, this will mean being honest about what we read, investigate, and watch, attending to the real reasons driving our intellectual reflection. We will have to learn to police our often-complicated desire to learn and distribute negative information about neighbors or celebrities and come to recognize the boundary between longing to know for the right reasons and the wrong ones. We will have to acquire discernment between the desire to view an especially explicit movie, television show, or book out of *curiositas* rather than upright concerns and even be willing to see that we sometimes shift from the latter to the former in the middle of our consumption. We will have to become comfortable with not knowing the latest gossip, even if our neighbors and colleagues take them to be critical pieces of information. This is, at least in part, what it means to apply Christian humility to our minds and hearts.

LEARNING WITHOUT THE END IN MIND AND SEEKING WHAT IS BEYOND US

So far, we have seen how longing to know can be a form of distracting us from our proper ends and of pressing us toward gaining illicit knowledge that threatens our well-being as God's image-bearing creatures. In both cases, humility can help us address these dangers by prompting us to respond rightly to our status as finite and fallen creatures. But Thomas also notes that our desire for knowledge can go awry in at least two more ways, which we will consider together in this section: when we seek knowledge without a consciousness of God's presence and when we seek to know what is beyond our capacity.

To help us understand this side of *curiositas*, let me share the story of a good friend, who happens to be one of the most thoughtful and studious people I know. As a child, my friend was notorious for wanting to know anything and everything, to the point that her family took to calling her "nosy Rosie." She was not only a voracious reader and learner but also an expert eavesdropper. When there was a conversation happening nearby that she knew she was not supposed to hear, she would surreptitiously take up a position that would allow her to pick up on the most interesting tidbits. There was nothing obviously malevolent in her desire to know—she was not seeking to find out secrets to blackmail her siblings or embarrass her parents. She just had an unbridled longing to know whatever she could read, see, or hear, and to read, see, and hear as much as she could.

But one day, this all changed as she found herself eavesdropping on her parents as they discussed a tragic miscarriage experienced by friends. The details were disturbing and sad and were especially traumatizing for a young child. Suddenly, she realized that she had transgressed a boundary she should not have crossed and for the first time regretted longing to know everything around her.

If you're anything like me, this story will leave you feeling conflicted. To some degree, we have been convinced by our culture that knowledge is always superior to ignorance and that being uninformed is one of the most dangerous ways to live. As a teacher, I regularly assess my students based on their interest and engagement in learning about the material we are studying, rewarding the curious students with more encouragement and better recommendations than their incurious counterparts. So I find myself looking askance at the moral the story is designed to reveal: namely, that we are not so unlike children, sometimes yearning for knowledge for which we were not designed.

But Scripture has a remarkably similar story at its very foundation. In the garden of Eden, God sets the stage for perfect human flourishing: all creation has been made good, and the Lord has wrought beautiful order that stands in stark contrast to the chaotic waters mentioned in Gen 1:1. It is a context of absolute abundance in which every human need—food, shelter, friendship, and communion with God—is fully met.

And yet even in this context of perfect flourishing, there is something for which humans are not designed—a tree whose fruit is not suitable to the condition of creaturely hearts. Both Jewish and Christian scholars have had fascinating debates for millennia about what the fruit of the tree of the knowledge of good and evil represents. A popular view for many centuries was that it had to do with sexual awakening, since Adam and Eve's eyes are opened to their nakedness soon after the incident, though this view is unlikely.[7] A more defensible proposal suggests that "good and evil" is a Semitic idiom intended simply to mean "everything." On this view, our first parents' temptation is to seek to acquire the omniscience that is appropriate only to their creator.[8] Perhaps the most common view asserts that the "knowledge of good and evil" represents moral discernment—the ability to know what is right and what is wrong.

But while this view has no trouble making sense of a literal reading of the story, it introduces a puzzling notion: that God would seek to keep humans from possessing the ability to discern between good and evil. After all, isn't this exactly the kind of knowledge which we generally want to seek? A case in point

7. This view has trouble making sense of Gen 3:22, in which God states that "the man has become like one of us in knowing good and evil." Most problematically, however, God has already warranted sexual union and blessed it in Gen 2:24, where man and woman are instructed to become "one flesh."

8. The primary weakness of this view, in addition to the paucity of attestation throughout the Old Testament and in other ancient Near Eastern literature, is that humans obviously did *not* gain universal knowledge. We continue to know only in part (1 Cor 13:9). For an overview of this view and its proponents, see Hamilton, *Book of Genesis*, 165.

is King Solomon, who asks for "an understanding mind . . . that I may discern between good and evil" (1 Kgs 3:9). God is undeniably pleased and grants him "a wise and discerning mind" (3:12). Given this and other similar narratives throughout Scripture, it's hard to see how the message of Gen 3 could be that humans ought not seek moral discernment.

A more compelling interpretation is to understand the Genesis narrative as making the claim that humans are creatures designed with a particular end in mind and that this *telos* (originally a Greek word that means "intended end or goal") must govern our quest for wisdom. Genesis is clear about what humanity is designed for—of all the creatures God made, Adam and Eve are the only ones who are called God's "images." In the ancient Near East, this language evoked notions of royalty and sonship; our first parents were designed to be representative rulers of the creation, governing territory that belonged to their Father and creator.[9]

The problem that emerges in Gen 3 is that Adam and Eve sought a kind of equality with God that was inconsistent with their nature, calling, and telos. Rather than imaging God as finite, dependent creatures, they made an experiment in self-government that would end in ruinous disaster. In this framing, then, the "knowledge of good and evil" is a kind of moral autonomy—a quest to be the arbiter of right and wrong, rather than submitting to the moral framework given by their creator.[10]

Humility and Embracing Our Creaturely Purpose

What does all of this have to do with humility in the information age? I think we should pay attention to two ideas here, each aligned with Thomas's two final warnings about our quest for knowledge. First, remember that Thomas warns his students against trying to learn about God's creatures without reference to God himself. This point makes sense only if, like Thomas, we share the conviction

9. For a rich and readable reflection on this concept in Old Testament perspective, see Imes, *Being God's Image*.

10. For further discussion, see Hamilton, *Book of Genesis*, 165–66.

that humans are made with a particular telos and that all of our activities should be shaped by that design: namely, for life with God. So whether we are reading a novel for fun, analyzing bacteria under a microscope, or listening to a good piece of music, we should conceive of these experiences as ultimately leading us toward our end—knowing God more fully.

If this sounds onerous—like someone on a self-righteous kick who can't just enjoy some literature or music like a normal person—it's not supposed to be. Instead, this perspective should dignify all of our activities, mundane as they may seem, by framing them as a part of following Jesus and knowing God better. Rather than dulling our ability to enjoy God's world, it should enhance it.

In fact, it's when we live without this telos in mind that we wind up spending our life at work and at home as if God didn't matter. We consider God's presence only in moments where we are praying for his assistance or attending church functions. This is what Thomas warned against when he said that we could too easily learn about the world without reference to its maker and our telos. Learning should always be a quest to know God's world in companionship with the very maker and sustainer of the cosmos.

This leads us to the second implication of the Genesis story and to Thomas's final warning: that we should not seek what is beyond us. When Adam and Eve seek to be "like God," they are not only ignoring their telos; they are aspiring to *be* and *know* what they cannot. This theme arises again in Gen 11, when the peoples of the earth seek to reach heaven, to "make a name" for themselves, and to resist the fulfillment of the divine command to fill the earth.

The theme continues to repeat throughout the Old Testament storyline, such as when Israel desires a king. The prophet Samuel warns that such rulers will inevitably seek to take for themselves the kind of sovereignty that only rightfully belongs to YHWH (1 Sam 8:10–18). Along the same lines, Isaiah reminds Israel of YHWH's fundamental difference from his creatures: "My thoughts are not your thoughts," we read, and "my ways are higher than your ways" (Isa 55:8–9). In the context, this statement is not an instance of divine boasting; instead, it is the basis of a call to repentance—the point is that Israel should stop trying to be its own god and submit to divine, saving grace for their own good.

This theme finds its culmination in Phil 2, where we hear a version of the Adam and Eve story that goes right instead of wrong. Whereas our first parents were not equal to God but sought to be, the uncreated Son of God—who *was* equal to God—chooses not to count his glory as "a thing to be grasped" (Phil 2:6). Here, Paul is taking up an aspect of Jesus's life that the Gospel writers also highlight: that Jesus is a new Adam, succeeding where the first Adam failed (Matt 4:1–11; Mark 1:12–13; Luke 4:1–13).[11] In the person of Jesus, we see how humans can rightly reflect their Creator, functioning as images of God: when we embrace the limits of humanity through obedient submission, rather than exalting ourselves and seeking what is beyond our capacity.

CONCLUSION—WHAT WOULD THOMAS DO?

At various times in Christian history, the warning against curiosity has been misconstrued in dangerous ways. Historically, it has sometimes been the basis of anti-intellectualism and anti-scientism: "If God wanted us to know about X [the human genome, the outer edges of the universe, etc.]," the argument goes, "he would have plainly revealed it. We should not try to 'play God' and see what is beyond our capacity."

This is a distortion of the point made in Scripture. After all, when Adam and Eve, or Israel, are rebuked, it is not because they were seeking to understand creation better, cure a disease, or develop new scientific theories. Instead, they were making idols out of knowledge of one kind or another; they were seeking a kind of autonomy to which humans are not properly suited.

To avoid the mistakes of previous generations, we should insist that humility not be misunderstood as a prohibition against all or even most kinds of curiosity; nor is it an essentially or even primarily a constraining force on our knowledge seeking. Instead,

11. Paul offers a summary of this "new Adam" theme in Rom 5:12–21.

it is the habit of heart and mind that provides a positive vision and a suitable space for cultivating the right kinds of curiosity. Thus, humility offers us not just a vision of consuming less knowledge but of cultivating an appetite for wisdom that allows us to pursue all of our knowing within the context of our status as creatures before God. This is precisely why Scripture describes the fear of the Lord—creaturely humility—as "the beginning of wisdom" (Prov 1:7): humility not only prevents us from pursuing what we should not seek to know but also puts us on the path to focus our limited energies on what matters most.

Were Thomas Aquinas alive today, I think he would genuinely rejoice at the abundance of knowledge humans have managed to cultivate over the last few centuries. I can imagine him poring over scientific journals, interacting with emerging literature and philosophy, and even playing around with ChatGPT. In his day, Thomas led the way in terms of trying to understand the natural world as best he could, including by recovering the work of Aristotle, a Greek philosopher whose thought was clearly at odds with Christian teaching in important ways.

What the example of Thomas teaches is that humility is not at odds with a rich, curious life but is in fact its cornerstone. Without humility, our search for knowledge will be scattered, misguided, and self-indulgent—a recipe for disaster in our current era of superabundant and super-accessible information. But armed with humility, an inquiring mind can find not only knowledge but wisdom. In short, humility empowers us to learn what is truly worth learning and tethers us more closely to God, who is the source of all wisdom and goodness.

Conclusion

Learning to Bake Humble Pie

In the cells of a Christian monastery situated on a rocky outcropping about halfway between Rome and Naples, a quiet revolution was underway. Benedict, the monastery's young and gifted leader, was composing a basic set of instructions to help the monks under his care pursue a life of faithful discipleship to Jesus of Nazareth. As he drew from previous Christian authors and reflected on Scripture himself, he ended up composing a "rule of life" that would wield enormous influence for centuries to come. The little book contained all kinds of practical advice about how to manage life in a Christian monastic community, but its crowning achievement was an explanation of how and why to cultivate the virtue of humility.

We don't know much for certain about Benedict's early life, even though he stands as a pivotal figure in the history of Christianity. He grew up on his family's estate about one hundred miles from Rome during the waning days of a unified Roman Empire, a season in which the Christian church would take on increasing importance as a stable institution in a world of rapid change and dissolution. Equally importantly, Benedict lived at a time when monasticism—a way of life focused on intentional living "alone or in a community under a rule of life and vows that give shape to [one's] daily routine and shared mission"[1]—was gaining strength but also in need of crucial guidance. As Christian monasteries

1. Peters, *Story of Monasticism*, 4.

increasingly dotted the landscape of Europe and Asia, questions abounded about how they should run. Should monks live in community or focus on solo prayer and reflection? Should they eat and sleep as little as possible, even to the point of damaging their health, or should there be some moderation even in their pursuit of all-out holiness?

Addressing these pressing questions, Benedict's rule was the right book at the right time. Historians often point out that more than other rules that had come before, Benedict's guidebook was both balanced and flexible, allowing it to be contextualized and adopted in a wide variety of circumstances. But this makes it perhaps too easy to overlook another reason for Benedict's success: namely, its focus on humility as a habit of heart and mind peculiarly suited to the task of following Jesus faithfully. Indeed, of its seventy-three chapters, the longest by far is the one focused on humility.

Because of the wild success of his rule, Benedict was almost certainly the most influential author to set down practical guidance regarding how to cultivate humility. But he was by no means the first or the only. From Christianity's earliest years, pastors and teachers recognized both the importance and the great difficulty of cultivating humility and developed patterns of behavior that could help them consistently pursue it. These guidelines were never intended as simplistic formulas that would allow one to obtain humility automatically. Nor were they considered to be effective as mere efforts of human righteousness. Instead, like exercises designed to strengthen the body, they were part of Christian efforts to develop habits that could help us in growing our "humility muscles."

So far, we've focused our attention primarily on the benefits of cultivating humility as modern people committed to trying to follow Jesus well. We've seen that despite the risks attendant to it, humility is a trait worth our attention and pursuit in the contemporary world (ch. 1). We've observed the importance of defining humility in biblical and Christological terms, since humility wrongly conceived has the terrible power to destroy rather than build up (ch. 2). We've applied that biblical and Christological account of humility to the tricky problems of evaluating our self-worth (ch. 3), sharing our religious convictions (ch. 4), and navigating a world of information superabundance (ch. 5). In each case, I hope you've been persuaded that cultivating biblical and Christ-shaped humility is a critical aspect of living a flourishing life of discipleship to Jesus of Nazareth and one that we can understand better when we turn to Scripture and early Christian writers.

In this chapter, we turn to the next critical question: Assuming we are convinced that humility is worthy of our pursuit, how do we go about cultivating it? To answer this question, we will consider Benedict's rule alongside other similar documents from leaders throughout Christian history. Many of these documents were written for people living out a vocation of monasticism in the premodern world, and so we will consider what it might look like to apply their insights in the twenty-first century as people who are not called to a life of monastic contemplation. As we'll see, despite our historical and cultural distance, the obstacles to and opportunities for cultivating humility remain largely the same as for our premodern forebears.

We'll organize the discussion around three principles that Benedict and other early church leaders focused on when giving practical guidance toward humility: (1) remembering our creatureliness, (2) recalling our sinfulness, and (3) cultivating intimacy with the humble Christ. In each case, we'll look not only at Benedict's specific advice but also at other early Christian sources that help us see what it looks like to pursue humility along these three lines in the modern world.

REMEMBERING OUR CREATURELINESS

I am nothing but dust and ashes. (Gen 18:27 NIV)

Across the Christian tradition, there is a consistent conviction about cultivating humility: it begins first of all with embracing our status as finite creatures who live and serve in the presence of an infinite and sovereign God. This emphasis on humility as fear of

God and awareness of his presence is one of the most important threads throughout the earliest known collections of monastic sayings.

Known simply as the sayings of the Desert Fathers, these texts assembled scores of proverbs and short stories gathered from leading lights of the first generations of Christian monks.[2] It was these collections that would form the foundation for the core teachings of future generations of monks, including Benedict, as they offered basic instruction about pursuing the difficult but rewarding path of discipleship to Jesus. Today, the Desert Fathers continue to inspire Christians seeking to follow Jesus well, whether in deserts, cities, or suburbs.[3]

Such is the centrality of humility for these early monks that John Wortley, a leading expert on the Desert Fathers, writes, "It is no exaggeration to say that humility is the very keystone and lynchpin of the Desert Fathers' teaching."[4] These monks believed that without both humility and fear of the Lord, the hard labor of the monastic life is entirely in vain. Long before the age of Christian celebrities—and their tragic downfalls—these monks had learned that even the most impressive spiritual leaders could be brought to nothing by the sin of pride and indeed that spiritual pride is most likely to creep in just as we are making significant spiritual progress.[5]

To make themselves less susceptible to pride, they emphasized a single-minded focus on God's presence and, in turn, our status as creatures who are always before him. Thus, the very first statement in a major collection of sayings from the Desert Fathers is this simple advice: "Wherever you go, keep God in mind."[6] Benedict built on this tradition, explaining that "the first step of

2. For an accessible translation of many of these sayings, see Ward, *Desert Fathers.*

3. For example, see Henri Nouwen's popular book *The Way of the Heart.*

4. Wortley, *Introduction to Desert Fathers*, 13.

5. Wortley, *Introduction to Desert Fathers*, 12–15; Ward, *Desert Fathers*, 148–70.

6. Ward, *Desert Fathers*, 3.

humility, then, is that a man keeps the fear of God always before his eyes (Ps 35[36]:2) and never forgets it."[7]

Here Benedict and the other monks mince no words: anyone who wants to follow Jesus will get nowhere unless they first cultivate an increasing awareness of and reverence toward their maker. Inversely, Benedict and the early monks recognized that pride thrives when we forget about God's presence and try to pursue life on our own terms. As a result, there is nothing more important than finding habits of life that can reliably cultivate awareness of our creatureliness and God's infinite greatness.

The Practices of Solitude and Silence

To achieve this aim, the monks commended a variety of practices, but they emphasized two in particular: solitude and silence. Why this supreme focus on finding quiet? In part, it surely had to do with what they saw in their savior: Jesus's ministry is often marked by intermittent periods of silence and solitude, as he and his disciples seek out "desolate" places to pray (e.g., Matt 14:13; Mark 1:35, 45; Luke 4:1–13; 4:42; 5:16).

But it was also because they recognized that solitude is often the only way to eliminate the noises and distractions of ordinary life that so frequently prevent us from reckoning with our status as creatures and our relationship with our creator. Even in the fourth and fifth centuries, apparently, life in a village or small city was replete with opportunities for distraction—activities or objectives that are not bad in themselves, but which had the effect of minimizing awareness of God.

If distraction was a problem fifteen hundred years ago, we should be very afraid; the modern world is, without doubt, a far more challenging context to cultivate a robust awareness of God's presence. Even as technology has granted us increasing leisure time, it also works to keep us perpetually tethered to work and social communities or to keep us entertained enough that we need

7. Benedict, *RB 1980*, 31.

never experience silence. As we saw in chapter 4, this often allows us to fill ourselves with more and more knowledge but less and less wisdom. Yet here we can also add another, deeper risk: a life of constant connection and distraction threatens to starve us from our source of life in God himself. In short, if our spiritual forefathers needed to practice solitude to help them stay connected with and aware of God, we surely need it more.

Importantly, the Christian monastic tradition did not commend total and unstructured isolation from others but instead focused on creating communities that would allow disciples of Jesus to pursue a life of single-minded devotion to Christ and sought to equip them with habits and practices that would help them use their solitude and silence well. In its healthiest forms, these seasons of monastic solitude were designed ultimately to equip Christians for missional service to others. As Greg Peters explains: "What these monks and nuns sought (and obtained on occasion) was an environment that gave them the opportunity and privilege of pursuing God in a less distracted manner, an environment conducive to a single-minded pursuit of God. Just as Jesus frequently retreated to isolated places to pray, so too have monastics throughout the centuries."[8]

It may be the case that some people will have both the calling and the ability to pursue extended periods of solitude like early monks. But for most people reading this book, it will be more practical and appropriate to pursue solitude and silence in smaller ways that can still be powerful and effective. Here are three very simple ways to start.

A Day Away

First, consider scheduling a one- or two-day retreat to create an extended time of solitude and silence. The power of these extended times away from people—and the devices that keep us connected to the world even when we could be alone—is that they can

8. Peters, *Story of Monasticism*, 40.

shake us out of the ruts and bad habits that we've unconsciously developed in our daily lives. Often, it's only after a full day away from our constant connection to other people and the internet that we discover a heightened awareness of how disconnected and unaware of God we have become in our daily rhythms. Finding solitude and quiet need not be expensive or extreme.

In the Filipino evangelical churches in which I grew up, relatively young and resource-poor Christian communities invested in simple rooms where people could find extended time with the Lord. This practice seems to be more common in many churches in the Majority World, perhaps because Christians in these contexts have started to follow Jesus after first being part of religious traditions that prioritize devoted, silent communion with God.

But if you can't find a dedicated space for your time away, this need not be a hindrance. If you live in a city, you can find solitude in a library or a church. If you can easily access some natural environment—a park, a forest, a beach, or just your own backyard—even better, since creation has a way of reminding us of our smallness and God's greatness and therefore helps build our humility muscles.

For these extended times away, you'll want to come prepared with a plan. As the monks who pioneered these practices attest, silence is a place where we meet God, but it's also where we come face-to-face with the enemy and all his wiles. So I recommend using a good resource such as Richard Foster's *Celebration of Discipline*, which has been helpful to Christians all over the world since it was written over four decades years ago.[9]

Daily Solitude and Silence

For some of us, life circumstances will not allow for even a day or two away from people. Some of us are caring for young children or elderly parents, for example, while others have jobs that offer little opportunity for extended rest. In these cases—and even for those

9. Readers may also benefit from a more recent book in the same vein: Comer, *Ruthless Elimination of Hurry.*

who can do longer retreats—a daily practice of solitude can be a crucial help in allowing us to connect with God and remember our status as his creatures. Christians through the centuries have most often found this to work well first thing in the morning, at a midday break, or just before bed. Whatever time it may be, even a few minutes of genuine solitude can make a significant impact in our cultivation of humility if we can really set aside our devices and our connections with others.

The key to these shorter times of quiet is to make the most of the time we have, allowing our status as God's creatures to sink in as we connect with him. A very practical way to use these shorter times of solitude and silence is to pray the Lord's Prayer. For millennia, Christians have found that this prayer offers a rich seedbed for cultivating life with God. It's also a perfect tool for cultivating humility, since it reminds us of our finitude and fallenness. In the first half of the prayer, we acknowledge God as God and confess our dependence upon him—reminding us that we are but dust. In the second half of the prayer, we seek God's forgiveness and ask for his help in our spiritual battles—more on this shortly.

Here is the bottom line: If we can cultivate *some kind* of daily habit of solitude and silence—if we allow our hearts to be drawn out of our self-imposed busyness—we open up a daily space for remembering our creatureliness and realigning ourselves with God's call to humble obedience.

Seeing and Embracing Silence in Daily Life

There is one more way that the monastic practices of solitude and silence can be woven into our lives, and it might be the best "on-ramp" to exercising our humility muscles. Before we try to schedule a day away or try to build a daily habit of solitude and silence, most of us should first consider simply embracing the silent moments that God presents to us in everyday life.

Modern life is, in some ways, constructed precisely with the goal of eliminating these moments of silence. While previous eras had built-in moments of quiet—waiting for a train or a bus, waiting for a friend to arrive, or waiting for your food to cook—we have worked relentlessly to eliminate all such gaps from our lives. Technology allows us to ensure we arrive at our destinations right on time and to create simple "instant" meals. The result is that most of us walk around totally unaccustomed to quiet, such that when we actually do encounter such moments by accident—perhaps we are stuck in traffic or have a longer-than-usual wait at the dentist—we feel a strong urge to fill the silence with some kind of noise.

I was struck by my own tendencies in this area when recently watching a YouTube video with my teenage son. This YouTube personality makes videos about himself going to strange places—poorly rated restaurants and hotels, for example—and trying things out while on camera. Typically, hilarity ensues.

In this video, he was trying out a sensory deprivation chamber, in which his task is to float in salt water in a darkened, isolated chamber, wearing soundproof earplugs. Apparently, such chambers have become a fad among affluent people who are longing for quiet (a longing that echoes in its own way the silence that the monks were seeking in the desert seventeen hundred years ago!). The YouTube star comments on the strangeness of the quiet and, after spending the first couple of hours in his typical, humorous mood, eventually starts to have a very emotional experience, openly weeping as he remembers his grandmother's quiet, diligent love for him as a child. It was definitely a more emotional video than the usual fare for this channel.[10]

Yet here is what was striking to me: the first thing he does after his time is up—even before he exits the sensory deprivation chamber—is check the notifications on his phone. My thought as I watched was how similar this has been to my own struggle to stay with silence and communion with God. One minute, I'm overwhelmed by a clear sense of God's presence, care, and faithfulness, learning a new spiritual lesson and finding a new aspect of some big truth. And the next minute I find myself drawn ineluctably back to the (usually) trivial emails and messages beckoning me. I wonder how much spiritual vitality do I say no to simply by

10. Trahan, "I Survived Sensory Deprivation."

refusing to accept the small silences that could otherwise be drawing my gaze higher and pulling my heart more toward humility and fear of the Lord.

As C. S. Lewis memorably puts it, "We are half-hearted creatures, fooling about with drink and sex and ambition [or social media pings] when infinite joy is offered us, like an ignorant child who wants to go on making mud pies in a slum because he cannot imagine what is meant by the offer of a holiday at the sea."[11] The only way to grasp "the weight of glory" is to develop a habit of embracing quiet time with and before God.

RECALLING OUR SINFULNESS

For I know my transgressions, and my sin is ever before me. (Ps 51:3)

So far, we have seen that Benedict and his fellow monks prioritized building humility through practices that remind us of our creatureliness. But this is only part of the story, since biblical humility grows from an awareness of not only our limitations but also our sin. It should be no surprise, then, to see that many of the monastic practices designed to help us grow our humility muscles were built around dealing well with sin.

In Benedict's rule, this takes two forms especially. First, as monks internalize the reality that we are always in God's presence, this should lead them to increased awareness of their own shortcomings before him. Thus, the rule explains that a monk must "recall that he is always seen by God in heaven, that his actions everywhere are in God's sight and are reported by angels at every hour," allowing him to guard himself "at every moment from sins and vices of thought or tongue, of hand or foot, of self-will or bodily desire."[12] Underscoring the importance of this idea, Benedict's command that monks be aware of sin—raised in the

11. Lewis, *Weight of Glory*, 2.

12. Benedict, *RB 1980*, 33.

first of Benedict's steps to humility—is treated again in his twelfth step. There, he urges a monk to judge himself "always guilty on account of his sins," and to "consider that he is already at the fearful judgment, and constantly say in his heart what the publican in the Gospel said with downcast eyes: Lord, I am a sinner, not worthy to look up to heaven (Luke 18:13)."[13] Second, Benedict commends supplementing this internal exercise with external practice: "The fifth step of humility is that a man does not conceal from his abbot any sinful thoughts entering his heart, or any wrongs committed in secret, but rather confesses them humbly."[14]

The Practice of Confessing Sin

The power of sin, temptation, and the devil were a subject of great fascination for the earliest Christian monks. They saw their pursuit of holiness as a spiritual battle against the broken and disordered desires we all develop as sinful humans and ultimately against the devil and demonic forces. As a result, they recognized that confession is not just an important part of spiritual hygiene but a powerful way of engaging in spiritual battle.

A story narrated by a young monk named Serapion illustrates the monks' conviction that confession plays a critical role in spiritual warfare. In the story, Serapion shares how as a young man, he began a habit of stealing bread after each group meal and then eating it secretly. "My conscience troubled me," he writes, "and I was ashamed to say anything to [the monk mentoring him] about it." One day, Serapion hears his supervisor explaining to someone else that "nothing harms the monk so much, and gives such happiness to the demons, as when he conceals his thoughts from his spiritual father." Serapion thinks that this is surely a reference to his own secret sin, which has somehow been found out, leading him to tearfully confess his sin and ask for forgiveness.

13. Benedict, *RB 1980*, 37–38.

14. Benedict, *RB 1980*, 36.

To his surprise and joy, his spiritual mentor tells him, "My son, you are set free from your captivity without me saying anything. You are freed by your own confession. The demon, which by your silence you let dwell in your heart, has been killed because you confessed your sin. You let him control you because you never said no to him, never withstood him. He will never make a home in you again, because you have thrown him out into the open." As he spoke, "Something like a flame shot out of my breast and so filled the house with its stench that the people present thought it was sulphur burning."[15]

Spectacular stories like these abound in the literature about the monks of this time. Whatever we may think of their credibility, we should not be surprised by their thrust, since Scripture itself lays out a similar way of thinking about confessing sin. In the most famous confession of sin in Scripture, Ps 51, David recognizes that it is only when he opens his heart to God fully that he can draw near and have true communion with the Lord. This picture is painted even more vividly in Ps 32, where David writes in vv. 3–4:

> For when I kept silent, my bones wasted away
> through my groaning all day long.
> For day and night your hand was heavy upon me;
> my strength was dried up as by the heat of summer.

David uses this vivid imagery here to describe an ironclad spiritual reality: when we avoid confession—choosing instead to minimize, distort, or simply ignore our sin—we wither and faint under its oppressive weight. It's only in openly confessing our sin that we, like David—and like young Serapion—can ward off the oppression of the enemy and rejoice in the Lord's steadfast love toward us (Ps 32:10–11). Just as crucially, Scripture also flags confession of sin as a prerequisite for receiving atonement and restored fellowship with God. In the Levitical Day of Atonement, the high point of the Mosaic law's treatment of sin and forgiveness, the high priest is told to "lay both his hands on the head of the live goat, and confess over it all the iniquities of the people of Israel, and all their

15. Ward, *Desert Fathers*, 23–24.

transgressions, all their sins" (Lev 16:21). In the New Testament, Christians are similarly called to confess their sins to God, walking as people of light rather than those trying to live in concealment (1 John 1:5–10). James also enjoins confessing our sins to others within the household of God (Jas 5:16).

So when Benedict encourages his readers to remain always aware of their sin, his aim is not to create a community of buzzkills or to cultivate a complex system of penance for Christians. Rather, he urges his fellow monks to take confession of sin utterly seriously because it is the only way to arrest a dreadful and inevitable chain reaction that develops in the absence of confession: forgetting our sins makes us forgetful of our need for God's help, and in this prideful soil, the works of the evil one have the perfect conditions to thrive. Leave a garden untended, and it will soon be nothing but weeds; leave a wound to fester, and deadly infections will ultimately harm the whole body; leave sin unconfessed, and it will overcome even the strongest Christ follower. Confession for the monks is thus a crucial tactic in combat with the forces of evil. As we bring sin into the light, its power over us is weakened, and the enemy's ability to tempt, shame, or otherwise oppress us is diminished.

It's important here to note that Christians have not always agreed about the nature of confession. During the Protestant Reformation, church leaders sought to correct practices of confession and penance that they believed had evolved in unhealthy directions. John Calvin, for example, expresses concern that requiring confession to priests as well as demanding elaborate rituals from those repenting ultimately subverts the proper goal of confession.[16] Rather than helping Christians draw near to God and be assured of their absolution as they bring their sins into the light, the church's practices had been undermining Christians' confidence in Christ's atoning work.

Even so, Calvin would likely be shocked at how little modern Christians practice personal and public confession of sin. His vision of this discipline involves regularly confessing sin fully and regularly to God, consistently confessing sin in the context of corporate

16. Calvin, *Institutes* 3.4.1–3.4.24.

worship, "disclosing our weaknesses to one another" so that we can pray for one another (Jas 5:16), and confessing to others we have wronged as part of biblical reconciliation (Matt 5:23–24).[17]

Calvin and the other Reformers hardly wanted to do away with confession of sin. Instead, they wanted to ensure that these practices actually worked to help Christians draw near to Christ, rather than oppressing them with human-made burdens and superstitions. Like Benedict, the Reformers recognized that the most crucial function of intentional confession of sin is to help us draw near to the triune God by humbling ourselves before him and, where appropriate, others. We forsake this humbling practice at our peril.

To sum up what we've said so far: Christians throughout the ages have found that certain practices can help us build our humility muscles. We've seen that monks like Benedict highlight three in particular: solitude, silence, and confession. These are by no means the only practices the monks and other Christians suggest. For example, we can add to these the disciplines of simplicity (avoiding excess in food, drink, and possessions), fasting (abstaining from food or drink for specified times), and joyful submission to authorities, all of which are crucial in Benedict's rule. In a recent and very good book, Gavin Ortlund adds several practical strategies to kill pride and cultivate humility. His list includes things like listening well, practicing gratitude, embracing criticism, and laughing at yourself.[18]

In this chapter, I've highlighted solitude, silence, and confession because I think they may be the most important practices in building our humility muscles. They have a unique way of making us more attentive to God's holy presence and more aware of our humble status as creatures who fall short of our design as his image bearers. They are keystone spiritual habits that can help ensure that the rest of our spiritual life can flourish.

They also happen to be three of the most countercultural humility-building habits. That is, despite being central to Christian

17. Calvin, *Institutes* 3.4.12.

18. Ortlund, *Humility*.

spirituality for most of our history, modern Christianity—and modern life in general—has largely left them behind. If the Desert Fathers or Benedict or Chrysostom or Calvin were brought to the present moment in a time machine, I think they would be genuinely surprised at how little time Christians spend using these practices to cultivate humility.

Yet as much as they would urge us to revive our appreciation and practice of these disciplines, I think they would want us to hear an even more crucial message. Despite their theological and vocational differences, they would unanimously tell us that whatever practices we adopt, they will be worthless unless we embrace them with a single-minded pursuit of communion with the humble Christ.

CODA: CULTIVATING INTIMACY WITH THE HUMBLE CHRIST

No one is a better guide here than Augustine, who understood well that while we learn humility through practices designed to increase our awareness of our finitude and fallenness, the doorway to such a life is entirely blocked until we come to know Jesus of Nazareth. Augustine knew about the quest to kill pride and cultivate humility in a very personal way. In fact, when he retells his life story in his *Confessions*, he lingers especially on the pride he carried as a learned, accomplished young man, having launched himself by sheer talent and wit from his far-flung North African roots to the elite echelons of Roman society. His quest to understand truth and beauty had led him to accept some general teachings of Christianity, but something held him back from committing to a life of fully trusting Jesus as savior and becoming a disciple.

He narrates in excruciating detail his soul's internal deliberations. He had learned enough to see that life with Jesus offers something infinitely better than any other way of life. He recognized in the lives of Christians a kind of transformation, fulfillment, and stable integrity that is far better than anything on offer from even the best philosophical and religious systems. He knew that the triune God was the only source of true enjoyment and that Jesus offers the only durable joy accessible to us as God's creatures.[19]

Yet he is held back again and again from committing to following Jesus because he knows that to follow the radical, humble Jesus will demand the same kind of radical humility of him. This was especially challenging because he took great pride in the wisdom and learning he had accumulated and enjoyed his status as a well-respected expert near the top of the social ladder.[20] As he puts it in one of his prayers, "I sought a way to obtain strength enough to enjoy you; but I did not find it until I embraced 'the mediator between God and man, the man Christ Jesus' (1 Tim 2:5). . . . To possess my God, the humble Jesus, I was not yet humble enough. *I did not know what his weakness was meant to teach.*"[21]

Ultimately, Augustine had to move from half-hearted faith that merely admired Jesus from afar to a position of genuine submission to him. And he saw that the doorway from his old way of life and this new one—the most crucial threshold for every human heart—is the humble Jesus, who offers a promise far better than any other. "Come to me," he says, "all you who are weary and burdened, and I will give you rest. Take my yoke upon you and learn from me, for I am gentle and humble in heart, and you will find rest for your souls" (Matt 11:28–29 NIV).[22] This message eventually melts Augustine's proud heart, and in his conversion, he experiences for the first time the rest that he has always been searching for.

Augustine spent the rest of his life seeking hard after the humble Jesus and pointing others to him. He became especially fond of Phil 2, the New Testament's richest humility text, citing it more than a thousand times throughout his writings.[23] There, Paul urges the Philippians to "do nothing from selfish ambition or conceit, but in humility count others more significant than yourselves"

19. Augustine, *Confessions* 7.17.23.

20. Augustine, *Confessions* 7.20.26.

21. Augustine, *Confessions* 7.18.24; emphasis added.

22. Augustine, *Confessions* 7.21.27.

23. Verwilghen, "Jesus Christ," 301.

(Phil 2:3). In the stunning Christ hymn of vv. 5–11, Paul goes on to call us to:

> Have this mind among yourselves, which is yours in Christ Jesus, who, though he was in the form of God, did not count equality with God a thing to be grasped, but emptied himself, by taking the form of a servant, being born in the likeness of men. And being found in human form, he humbled himself by becoming obedient to the point of death, even death on a cross. Therefore God has highly exalted him and bestowed on him the name that is above every name, so that at the name of Jesus every knee should bow, in heaven and on earth and under the earth, and every tongue confess that Jesus Christ is Lord, to the glory of God the Father.

As we saw in chapter 2, this passage is in some sense the culmination of the biblical picture of humility, bringing together the loose threads of the Old Testament and weaving them into a new tapestry based on the work of Jesus. Here we learn that to follow Jesus is to adopt the same humble mindset that we see in his life and death—something made possible for us precisely because we are united to Jesus through faith. Thus, as Augustine would put it in his sermons on the Gospel of John, Christ's humility is not only *an example for us to follow* (though it is certainly that); it is *the only life-giving medicine that can heal the swollen, self-focused human heart.*[24]

This insight—that humility is, above all else, about deep acquaintance with the humble Christ—is the big truth behind, below, and around everything we have been studying. It is true that humility is, in a sense, an observable phenomenon, susceptible to measurement by psychologists and investigation by philosophers and theologians. It is likewise true that, even if there may not quite be "formulas" for cultivating humility, there are practices that Christians throughout the ages have found reliable in guiding us toward it. Yet Augustine reminds us that beyond all this analysis, humility is not only a concept but a person. And the reward for

24. Augustine, *Homilies on John* 3.2 (*NPNF*[1] 7:19).

those willing to yield their allegiance to him is the richest prize of all: fellowship with the one in whom our restless and weary hearts find true solace.

Bibliography

Aquinas, Thomas. *Summa Theologica*. Translated by Fathers of the English Dominican Province. 22 vols. New York: Benziger Brothers, 1911–25.

Aristotle. *The Nicomachean Ethics*. Edited by Lesley Brown. Translated by David Ross. Oxford World's Classics. New York: Oxford University Press, 2009.

Augustine of Hippo. *Confessions*. Edited and translated by Henry Chadwick. Oxford World's Classics. New York: Oxford University Press, 2008.

———. *Homilies on the Gospel of John*. *NPNF*[1] 7:7–452.

———. *Letters*. *NPNF*[1] 1:209–593.

———. *On Nature and Grace: Against Pelagius*. *NPNF*[1] 5:116–51.

———. *On the Catechizing of the Uninstructed*. *NPNF*[1] 3:282–314.

———. *Teaching Christianity (De Doctrina Christiana)*. Edited by John E. Rotelle. Translated by Edmund Hill. The Works of Saint Augustine: A Translation for the 21st Century. Hyde Park, NY: New City, 1996.

———. *The Trinity (De Trinitate)*. Edited by John E. Rotelle. Translated by Edmund Hill. The Works of Saint Augustine: A Translation for the 21st Century. Hyde Park, NY: New City, 1991.

Bauckham, Richard. *God Crucified: Monotheism and Christology in the New Testament*. Grand Rapids: Eerdmans, 1999.

Baumeister, Roy F., et al. "Does High Self-Esteem Cause Better Performance, Interpersonal Success, Happiness, or Healthier Lifestyles?" *Psychological Science in the Public Interest* 4 (2003) 1–44.

Bellitto, Christopher M. *Humility: The Secret History of a Lost Virtue*. Washington, DC: Georgetown University Press, 2023.

Benedict. *RB 1980: The Rule of St. Benedict in English*. Edited by Timothy Fry et al. Collegeville, MN: Liturgical, 1981.

———. *The Rule of St. Benedict*. Edited by Timothy Fry et al. Vintage Spiritual Classics. New York: Vintage, 1998.

Bock, Darrell L. *Luke*. 2 vols. BECNT. Grand Rapids: Baker, 1994.

Branden, Nathaniel. *The Psychology of Self-Esteem: A Revolutionary Approach to Self-Understanding That Launched a New Era in Modern Psychology*. 32nd anniv. ed. San Francisco: Jossey-Bass, 2001.

Calvin, John. *Institutes of the Christian Religion*. Edited by John T. McNeill. Translated by Ford Lewis Battles. 2 vols. Philadelphia: Westminster, 1960.

Carr, Nicholas G. *The Shallows: What the Internet Is Doing to Our Brains*. New York: Norton, 2011.

Collins, Drew, et al., eds. *The Joy of Humility: The Beginning and End of the Virtues*. Waco, TX: Baylor University Press, 2020.

Collins, Jim. "Level 5 Leadership: The Triumph of Humility and Fierce Resolve." *Harvard Business Review* 79 (2001) 66–76.

Comer, John Mark. *The Ruthless Elimination of Hurry: How to Stay Emotionally Healthy and Spiritually Alive in Our Current Chaos*. London: Hodder & Stoughton, 2019.

Couenhoven, Jesse. "'Not Every Wrong Is Done with Pride': Augustine's Proto-Feminist Anti-Pelagianism." *SJT* 61 (2008) 32–50.

Dickens, Charles. *David Copperfield*. London: Bradbury & Evans, 1850.

Dickson, John P. *Humilitas: A Lost Key to Life, Love, and Leadership*. Grand Rapids: Zondervan, 2011.

Du Bois, W. E. B. "Of the Faith of Our Fathers." In *The Souls of Black Folk: Essays and Sketches*, 189–206. Chicago: McClurg, 1903.

Edwards, Dennis R. *Humility Illuminated: The Biblical Path Back to Christian Character*. Downers Grove, IL: InterVarsity, 2023.

The Episcopal Church. *The Book of Common Prayer and Administration of the Sacraments and Other Rites and Ceremonies of the Church*. Repr., New York: Oxford University Press, 1979.

Exline, Julie J., and Peter C. Hill. "Humility: A Consistent and Robust Predictor of Generosity." *Journal of Positive Psychology* 7 (2012) 208–18.

Foster, Richard J. *Celebration of Discipline: The Path to Spiritual Growth*. San Francisco: Harper & Row, 1978.

———. *Learning Humility: A Year of Searching for a Vanishing Virtue*. Downers Grove, IL: InterVarsity, 2022.

Gilroy, Dan, dir. *Nightcrawler*. Los Angeles: Open Road, 2014.

Hamilton, Victor P. *The Book of Genesis: Chapters 1–17*. NICOT. Grand Rapids: Eerdmans, 1990.

Hess, Edward D., and Katherine Ludwig. *Humility Is the New Smart: Rethinking Human Excellence in the Smart Machine Age*. Oakland: Berrett-Koehler, 2017.

Hilbig, Benjamin E., and Ingo Zettler. "Pillars of Cooperation: Honesty-Humility, Social Value Orientations, and Economic Behavior." *Journal of Research in Personality* 43 (2009) 516–19.

Holmes, Michael W., ed. and trans. *The Apostolic Fathers in English*. After the earlier version by J. B. Lightfoot and J. R. Harmer. 3rd ed. Grand Rapids: Baker Academic, 2006.

Hopkin, Cameron R., et al. "Intellectual Humility and Reactions to Opinions About Religious Beliefs." *Journal of Psychology and Theology* 42 (2014) 50–61.

Hume, David. *An Enquiry Concerning the Principles of Morals*. Edited by John B. Stewart. 2nd ed. La Salle, IL: Open Court, 1966.

Imes, Carmen Joy. *Being God's Image: Why Creation Still Matters*. Downers Grove, IL: IVP Academic, 2023.

James, William. *The Principles of Psychology*. Vol. 1. London: Macmillan, 1891.

Kempis, Thomas à. *The Imitation of Christ*. Translated by Aloysius Croft and Harold Bolton. Mineola, NY: Dover, 2003.

Kivistö, Sari. *The Vices of Learning: Morality and Knowledge at Early Modern Universities*. Education and Society in the Middle Ages and Renaissance 48. Boston: Brill, 2014.

Krause, Neal. "Assessing the Relationships Among Wisdom, Humility, and Life Satisfaction." *Journal of Adult Development* 23 (2016) 140–49.

Kristian, Bonnie. *Untrustworthy: The Knowledge Crisis Breaking Our Brains, Polluting Our Politics, and Corrupting Christian Community*. Grand Rapids: Brazos, 2022.

Kristjánsson, Kristján. *The Self and Its Emotions*. Studies in Emotion and Social Interaction. New York: Cambridge University Press, 2010.

Kross, Ethan, and Igor Grossmann. "Boosting Wisdom: Distance from the Self Enhances Wise Reasoning, Attitudes, and Behavior." *Journal of Experimental Psychology* 141 (2012) 43–48.

Leary, Mark R., et al. "Cognitive and Interpersonal Features of Intellectual Humility." *Personality and Social Psychology Bulletin* 43 (2017) 793–813.

Lewis, C. S. *The Weight of Glory: And Other Addresses*. New York: Macmillan, 1949.

McCracken, Brett. *The Wisdom Pyramid: Feeding Your Soul in a Post-Truth World*. Wheaton, IL: Crossway, 2021.

McElroy, Stacey E., et al. "Intellectual Humility: Scale Development and Theoretical Elaborations in the Context of Religious Leadership." *Journal of Psychology and Theology* 42 (2014) 19–30.

Newbigin, Lesslie. *The Open Secret: An Introduction to the Theology of Mission*. Rev. ed. Grand Rapids: Eerdmans, 1995.

Newton, John. "Amazing Grace." Hymnary, 1779. https://hymnary.org/text/amazing_grace_how_sweet_the_sound.

Nietzsche, Friedrich Wilhelm. *On the Genealogy of Morals*. Translated by Douglas Smith. Oxford World's Classics. New York: Oxford University Press, 1996.

Nouwen, Henri J. M. *The Way of the Heart: The Spirituality of the Desert Fathers and Mothers*. New York: HarperOne, 2009.

Ortlund, Gavin. *Humility*. Wheaton, IL: Crossway, 2022.

Pardue, Stephen. "Humility." *Brill Encyclopedia of Early Christianity Online*, 2018. https://doi.org/10.1163/2589-7993_EECO_SIM_00001639.

———. "Kenosis and Its Discontents: Towards an Augustinian Account of Divine Humility." *SJT* 65 (2012) 271–88.

———. *The Mind of Christ: Humility and the Intellect in Early Christian Theology*. New York: T&T Clark, 2013.

Peters, Greg. *The Story of Monasticism: Retrieving an Ancient Tradition for Contemporary Spirituality*. Grand Rapids: Baker, 2015.

Porter, Steven L., et al. "Religious Perspectives on Humility." In *Handbook of Humility: Theory, Research, and Applications*, edited by Everett L. Worthington Jr. et al., 47–61. New York: Routledge, 2016.

Rieger, Joerg. *Christ and Empire: From Paul to Postcolonial Times*. Minneapolis: Fortress, 2007.

Shepherd, Steven, and Kathryn Belicki. "Trait Forgiveness and Traitedness Within the HEXACO Model of Personality." *Personality and Individual Differences* 45 (2008) 389–94.

Smith, Laura L., and Charles H. Elliott. *Hollow Kids: Recapturing the Soul of a Generation Lost to the Self-Esteem Myth*. Roseville, CA: Prima Lifestyles, 2001.

Stackhouse, John G., Jr. *Humble Apologetics: Defending the Faith Today*. New York: Oxford University Press, 2002.

Trahan, Ryan. "I Survived Sensory Deprivation." YouTube video, Mar. 18, 2022. https://www.youtube.com/watch?v=Xh2TYoDMbas.

Turkle, Sherry. *Alone Together: Why We Expect More from Technology and Less from Each Other*. New York: Basic, 2011.

Verwilghen, Albert. "Jesus Christ: Source of Christian Humility." In *Augustine and the Bible*, edited and translated by Pamela Bright, 301–12. Bible Through the Ages. Notre Dame, IN: University of Notre Dame Press, 1999.

Ward, Benedicta, ed. *The Desert Fathers: Sayings of the Early Christian Monks*. Penguin Classics. New York: Penguin, 2003.

Whitcomb, Dennis, et al. "Intellectual Humility: Owning Our Limitations." *Philosophy and Phenomenological Research* 94 (2017) 509–39.

———. "The Puzzle of Humility and Disparity." In *The Routledge Handbook of Philosophy of Humility*, edited by Mark Alfano et al., 72–83. Routledge Handbooks in Philosophy. New York: Routledge, 2020.

Wollstonecraft, Mary. *"A Vindication of the Rights of Woman" and "A Vindication of the Rights of Men."* Edited by Janet Todd. Oxford World's Classics. New York: Oxford University Press, 1999.

Wortley, John, ed. and trans. *The Anonymous Sayings of the Desert Fathers: A Select Edition and Complete English Translation*. New York: Cambridge University Press, 2013.

———. *An Introduction to the Desert Fathers*. New York: Cambridge University Press, 2019.

Young, John H. *Our Deportment: Or, the Manners, Conduct, and Dress of the Most Refined Society*. Springfield, MA: King, 1882.

Zakrzewski, Vicki. "How Humility Will Make You the Greatest Person Ever." *Greater Good Magazine*, Jan. 12, 2016. https://greatergood.berkeley.edu/article/item/humility_will_make_you_greatest_person_ever.

Zhang, Hansong, et al. "Intellectual Humility and Forgiveness of Religious Conflict." *Journal of Psychology and Theology* 43 (2015) 255–62.

www.ingramcontent.com/pod-product-compliance
Lightning Source LLC
LaVergne TN
LVHW051008080826
845145LV00009B/2520

* 9 7 8 1 7 2 5 2 5 4 6 3 3 *